"I never fail to be amazed by the number of would-be self employed who engage in unprotected entrepreneurialism without the elementary safeguards against ri

If only the *ment For You?* Thi you? / anyone contempl covers it all from eckbook. This distillation of knowledge, wisdom and experience, presented in Casey's call-it-as-he-sees-it style, is a must addition to any budding entrepreneur's library. Don't start a business without it."

Alf Nucifora
Nucifora Consulting Group
Atlanta

Is

Self-Employment

for You?

"Anyone can start a business...
Only a few can sustain a business."

Paul E. Casey

HARA
PUBLISHING GROUP

Hara Publishing Group, Inc.
P.O. Box 19732
Seattle, WA 98109
425-775-7868

10 9 8 7 6 5 4 3 2

Printed in the United States of America

LCCN 2003115779
ISBN 1-887542-17-5

Cover Design: Laura Zugzda
Editor: Robert Lindsay
Proofreader: Vicki McCown
Contributor: Ryan Adams
Interior Layout: Stephanie Martindale

Contents

Additional Copies of Book and CD Available

Additional copies of this book can be ordered by turning to page 219.

There is also a separate or inclusive *Is Self-Employment for You?* CD available. Author Paul Casey narrates the major points of the book in a compelling, informative and easy to listen to 70-minute CD. Listen to the CD while driving to work or just relaxing at home. Who knows, maybe something you hear in the CD will jump start you into a new world of independence.

Dedication

All of the following people listed below have had a very positive influence on me at some point in my life and this book is dedicated to them. When making a list such as this, there is no question that someone very important will be omitted because of a temporary lapse in memory. For any omission, I apologize in advance and I will definitely pick you up in the second edition.

To my wife Marti, my father and mother, brothers Jim, Joe, and Bob, Lynn Casey, Kathy Casey, Janet Casey, Tom Casey, Vic Kucera, Dan Evans, Ken Luce, Larry Coffman, Lynn Richardson, Jerry Kane, Dr. Glenn Terrell, Norm & Constance Rice, Irv Stimpson, Tom O'Brien, Sherri Erickson, Lou & Diane Tice, Joe Miller, Greg & Sharon Nickels, John Wooden, John, Robert, and Edward Kennedy, Dr. Martin Luther King, Larry Adams, Ryan Adams, Joe Jacovini, Mike Sweeney, Darlene Lindberg, George Polley, Rob Shultz, Mike Price, Mark Backman, Jennifer James, Mark Holden, Diane Kolb, H. Dewayne Kreager, The Volz Family, Neil Peterson, Pete Delaunay, Tom Peters, Muhammad Ali, Reverand Dale Turner, Earl Boynton, Bo Dickey, Dr. Lane Rawlins, and many more incredible people who have supported me personally and have lit up my path along the way.

Introduction

If you are reading this book, it's likely that you are seriously thinking of starting your own business. Maybe you've already started your own home-based consulting practice or entrepreneurship, and you are looking for some tips on how to make it prosper. Either way, you've come to the right place.

This book is a compendium of the on-the-job lessons that I have learned in fifteen years as a self-employed business owner. The purpose of this book is to help you to determine if *you* are a good candidate for self-employment.

This book takes an in-depth look at the *emotional and personality traits* that make up the **Mindset** of a self-employed business owner. If you have these emotional and personality traits, then self-employment may be for you. This book also takes a close look at the choices you must make concerning your **Lifestyle** if you decide to start your own business.

This book may not be what you have come to expect from a business book. I have some theories about how to sustain a successful business that may be radically different from what you have previously heard or read. For example:

- I believe that many businesses fail because they have *too much money* in the beginning, rather than too little.

- I believe that the customer is *not* always right.

- I believe that competitors are your best friends.

- I believe that you should follow your passion—but that doesn't necessarily mean the *money* will follow.

- I believe that real entrepreneurs don't need partners.

It's a sad fact that many businesses fail within their first five years. Very often, the business owners had no idea what they were getting into when they started out. They were so in love with the idea of *having* a business, or with the *business concept* they had created, that they didn't take the time to find out what steps were *really* necessary to make their business grow. They learned the hard way that it takes more than just a "hot idea" to make a successful business.

> Anyone can start a business...only a few people can sustain a business, and keep it going for the long run.

The same applies to *you* and whatever type of business you wish to start. Your amazing Internet software package may be the greatest thing since sliced bread, but it is virtually useless if you don't know how to market it to the right people. Likewise, just because you make a mean taco in the kitchen at home, it doesn't necessarily follow that you can run a successful Mexican restaurant. Anyone can start a business...only a few people can sustain a business—and keep it going for the long run.

This book gives you practical advice about how to keep your business going once you've started it. My goal is to help you to create a business that will *succeed*—and furthermore, will succeed over the long term. This book shows you how to develop a good business mindset, and how to manage your own personal lifestyle so that it will be an asset, not a liability, to your business. It also tells you about the pitfalls that start-up businesses often fall into, and how to avoid them.

In this book, you'll learn about the choices, both professional and personal, that you must make in order to succeed as a self-employed business owner. You'll learn how to use common sense in your business decisions, how to organize your time efficiently, and how to use self-analysis and accountability to avoid fatal mistakes. You'll see how good professional and people skills can help you to develop long-term relationships with your clients...and also, believe it or not, with your competitors. You'll learn the basics of a simple but effective marketing campaign, the methods and advantages of keeping low overhead, and how to avoid the trap of taking on unnecessary profit-killing partners.

What this book *doesn't* give you is a lot of high-level business theory. This is not the short version of an M.B.A. (In case you're worried, an M.B.A. isn't an absolute must for starting a successful business. I'm living proof of that.) If you're looking for a book that will tell you how to create a business plan, deal with business-related taxes, etc., see the "Further Reading" section at the end of this book. There are some excellent books that deal with the ABCs of business, and I recommend that you read them after you finish this book.

But this book deals more with the *psychology* of being a self-employed business owner, and the day-to-day business decisions that you will make. This is the stuff they don't teach you in business school, the "street smarts" that you learn on the job. You may have heard an experienced businessman say, "If I knew back then what I know now, things would have gone a lot smoother for me." Well, this is me, an experienced businessman, telling you what I "know now," after fifteen years in business, so you don't have to learn certain things the hard way.

Be warned, I offer no easy business solutions, no "get-rich-quick" schemes. I can't tell you how to make $10 million in ten years. But if you follow the advice I give in this book, in three to five years you might have a business that is stable and working for you, providing you with a regular, healthy income. And you'll be able to sustain this business, through good times and bad, for as long as you like, whether it is ten years, twenty years, or until you retire (that is, if you even *want* to retire—and in this book, I'll talk about whether or not retirement should even be an option.)

After reading this book, you may ultimately decide that self-employment is *not* for you. That's perfectly fine! If you decide that it will be better for you to stick with a steady income, eight-to-five job, there's nothing wrong with that. Starting a business is a major commitment, and it is not for everyone. It takes a special mindset, a good deal of sacrifice, and more than a bit of extra work to be an entrepreneur.

Take it from me: If you have the right personality traits, self-employment can be an extremely-satisfying endeavor.

But if you have skills and experience that can translate well into a small business, are a self-starter, and are willing to make some adjustments to your own lifestyle in order to serve your business needs, your chances for long-term success as a self-employed business owner are very good. And the journey to a successful business, though rocky at times, is often rich and rewarding. Take it from me: If you have the right personality traits, self-employment can be an extremely satisfying endeavor.

CHAPTER ONE

———◆———

What Are Your Reasons?

Why do you want to start your own business?

You don't need this book to tell you that we live in an age of erratic business cycles and volatile market trends. Corporate employment no longer provides the same level of security or the same promise of success that it once did. It seems as if every day we hear a new report on the latest victims of Corporate America's declining business practices. Executives and stockholders now determine the fates of employees based not on the individual employee's value or job performance, but on the company's profits and losses. Workers lose their jobs, savings, and pensions to poor corporate leadership. In extreme cases such as Enron, Tyco, and WorldCom, major corporations with thousands of employees have incurred huge scandals, or even been forced out of business by the poor decision-making, reckless greed, and fraudulent business practices of their executives. Even in this unstable business climate, many people still think they have no choice but to keep working for someone else. Others who have managed to keep their jobs in spite of hard times are still quite satisfied with corporate employment.

But some people dream of being self-employed, of owning their own independent business. They want to break away from the boss, the company, or the industry in which they seem to be stuck in perpetual servitude. They want to escape the "rat race" of corporate employment and take control of their own destiny. They don't want someone else telling them how much money they are worth, what time they should come to work, when they can take vacations, eat lunch, take a break, etc. And those of us who are already self-employed hope to stay in business long enough to see the fruits of our labors.

This book identifies the critical personality traits that are necessary for self-employment.

If you are reading this book, you probably have a strong desire for the independence of self-employment. Again, the purpose of this book is to give you an accurate sense of your prospects for success as an entrepreneur. This book identifies the critical personality traits that are necessary for self-employment.

If you do join the ranks of the self-employed, rest assured you will not be alone. The number of self-employed workers and free agents in the American workforce is growing so rapidly that no one is quite sure how many there are now or will be in the near future. For example, the American Association of Home-Based Businesses recently counted over 24 million home businesses in the United States. The Home-Based Business Owners Association puts the number at 27 million. And in the year 2000, the business research group IDC predicted that the number of home-based businesses would surpass 37 million by the year 2002.

In addition, there is a growing section of the workforce known variously as "soloists," "freelancers," or "independent professionals" who have no single employer, and who regularly move from job to job, from contract to contract. The Aquent Index, an annual survey of independent workers, recently counted over 33 million people in this category, or roughly one-fourth of the American workforce. Clearly, anyone who wishes to become self-employed will find themselves in good company.[1]

[1] Previous statistics quoted in *Free Agent Nation*, by Daniel H. Pink, published by Warner Books, Inc.

WHY GO INTO BUSINESS FOR YOURSELF?

The most basic step of self-employment—deciding to start a business—is not as simple as it seems. It's easy to say, "Okay, I'll just start my own business," quit your job, and plunge right in. Easy, but very foolish. Before you decide to become an entrepreneur, you should answer this question: **"*Why* do I want to start my own business?"**

I firmly believe that you must have some deep and very strong reasons for wanting to be self-employed. Only *you* can say for yourself what those reasons are. Hopefully, you are starting a business for the *right* reasons:

> *Good Reason:* I want to control my own destiny, both intellectually and financially.
> *Bad Reason:* I'm tired of wearing a suit and tie to work. I want to be able to work at home in bermuda shorts.

> *Good Reason:* I have a great concept, and I have the experience that it will take to turn this concept into a profitable and successful business.
> *Bad Reason:* I'm a great cook, so I think I will open a restaurant.

> *Good Reason:* I want to slowly but surely build a small business that will provide long-term security for myself and my family, a business that will keep going even through the hard times.
> *Bad Reason:* I want to cash in on the latest Internet business fad, create my own web company, and make a million dollars within one year.

There was a day not long ago when people went into business for all the right reasons. Usually, it was because they had an idea or a dream that they wanted to build into a successful, long-term enterprise. They may have had an original business concept or a brilliant discovery that the world had never seen before. Or, their business might have been something more ordinary, like a farm, a barbershop, a retail store, a dry-cleaning service, a visiting maid service, or an engineering firm. These businesses were nothing mind-boggling, but they did provide the entrepreneur with more freedom, more money, and more time. It wasn't about IPO's or how much money a company could return on investment to stockholders. It was called capitalism.

Just because you make a good pizza, it doesn't mean you can run a successful pizzeria. Just because you're a great artist, it doesn't mean you can run an art gallery.

But having a dream is only half the coin. I agree with half the saying, "Follow your passion, and the money will follow." Follow your passion? Yes! The money will follow? Not necessarily.

Turning your passion into a profit is a remarkable achievement, and it will certainly help you to keep your business going through hard times if you enjoy the work that you do. But be aware that *having a passion* and *turning that passion into a successful business* are two different things. In other words, don't confuse the dream with the *reality*.

Self-employment is about more than following your passion. In the end, it's about developing and executing *business systems* that work over the long run. It's all about getting cash, so it can flow. It's about paying your vendors on time and making sure that you are square with the tax man. It's about paying your rent, meeting deadlines, and juggling numerous tasks at once. It's about keeping your overhead low and staying out of debt. (As dull as it sounds, General Electric and Microsoft Corporation will only survive if they bring in more dollars at the end of the year than they spend. This is a basic goal for any business, but how often is this goal violated or not met?)

It's very important to believe in yourself and your product or service if you want your business to be successful in the long run. If you are just "in it for the money," it will be much harder to succeed. As a self-employed business owner, you will go through many highs and lows both financially and emotionally. Your ultimate goal is to have the highs not so high and the lows not too low. You want to achieve *consistency*.

Having strong reasons for starting your own business will help you to get through the difficult times. When I wasn't making a steady income, it helped that I believed strongly in what I was doing. Below is a list of my primary reasons for starting my own business. As a marketing and communications specialist, the clients that I serve and the type of work that I do have changed dramatically over the last fifteen years. What has never changed are my basic reasons for wanting my own business.

MY FIVE MAJOR REASONS

Here are the reasons why I, Paul E. Casey, want to own my own business:

1. I want to develop a successful communications business. As part of my business, I want to employ a creative and extremely competent communications team made up of free agents to serve the needs of my clients.

2. I want freedom of my time.

3. I want freedom of expression and association.

4. Using the latest communications technology, I want to create a virtual office that will allow me to conduct my business anytime, anywhere.

5. I want to achieve financial independence.

Let's take a quick look at where I am now in meeting these goals. Have I fulfilled my five reasons?

REASON #1: Over fifteen years ago, I created my own independent communications firm, Casey Communications, located
in Seattle, Washington. What started out as a small publishing
firm has evolved into a successful media buying business. I specialize in buying air time for clients who wish to advertise on
the radio. As part of my service, I study the demographics for
over 150 radio markets across the country to determine where
my client's best target audience lives. I create radio commercials for my clients and buy air time from radio stations to broadcast those commercials. As part of my business, I employ a team
of free agents to handle the writing, production, and distribution of the radio commercials.

**A clear and
specific definition
of the kind of
business that you
want to create.**

In fifteen years of owning my
own business, I have gained a
good reputation for providing
my clients with broadcast and
print services, creative advice
and placement. If a company
wants to market its services to
the general public, I would like them to come to me. My clients
have included everyone from retirement centers to travel agencies, and from small and medium-sized businesses to Fortune
500 companies.

This first reason is the most crucial of the five. It explains in a
nutshell what my business is and what my overall goals are for
the business itself. I believe that everyone who wishes to start
their own business should have a similar "first reason." In other
words, your "first reason" for wanting to go into business for
yourself should be a clear and specific definition of the kind of
business that you want to create.

REASON #2: I am in the process of achieving freedom of time.
I believe that, like many goals in life, freedom of time is something that you must work for continuously. To me, freedom of
time means spending as much time as possible doing the things

I enjoy, whether it's owning and operating my own business, or spending time with my family and friends.

As a self-employed business owner, I am master of my own work schedule. I can set my own pace and schedule the time to get my work as I see fit. This does not mean, of course, that I can sit back and relax in my office every day. Running a business always takes a great deal of effort. But I don't have anyone else telling me that I have to clock in by 8 AM, have lunch from noon to 1 PM, and clock out at 5 PM.

Freedom of time also means I am free to travel whenever I want to. One reason I went into the communications business was that I knew it would give me opportunities to travel while still conducting business. If I had opened a small retail store that required my presence every day, traveling would have been a lot more difficult.

REASON #3: It's very important for me to be able to express my opinions about politics, world events, the economy, etc., without fear of repercussions. We live in a country where freedom of speech is a cherished right. Freedom of expression is more important to me than money. I'm not suggesting that I am free to express *any* opinion I have whenever I want to, but I am closer to that goal today than I have ever been before.

I am also achieving freedom of association. As a self-employed business owner, I have the freedom to seek out my own clients. I also have the freedom to *refuse* to work with clients whom I don't want to work with. If I sense that a client is not quite ethical in their business practices, if I don't like their attitude (e.g., they try to talk me down on my fee), or if I don't feel that they really need my service (perhaps their business is not yet ready for radio advertising), I have the freedom to turn them down.

REASON #4: I have created my own virtual office that enables me to conduct my business anytime, anywhere. My wife and I are going to Hawaii this week. I will take my laptop computer and cell phone with me, so I will be able to stay in touch with my important clients in case they need me.

During my vacation, I will check e-mails and voice-mails twice a day. I don't anticipate having to work more than thirty minutes on any given day. Thanks to my virtual office, I've been able to take over two months of vacation this year. While I'm away from the physical office, my business will continue to run via an assortment of free agents. I have enough confidence in these agents to know they will keep things running smoothly in my absence.

When people who work eight-to-five jobs hear I am taking my cell phone and laptop with me to Hawaii, they think I am a workaholic who can't get away from his business. But when these people go on their annual two- to three-week vacation, they are generally so burned out that they want nothing to do with their company or profession.

Because I enjoy what I do, it does not cause me any distress to keep in touch with my business clients while I'm on the road. Notice I say "distress," not "stress." For me, "stress" is that tension and stimulation you feel when you are working on events within your control. In many ways stress is a good thing; it gives you a reason to get out of bed in the morning. "Distress," on the other hand, is the tension you feel when events are out of your control. Mind you, this doesn't necessarily mean that events *are* out of control, only that *you* are feeling tension because you can't be there to control them. In other words, "distress" is what you feel when events are controlling you. Having a virtual office keeps me from feeling distress because it enables me to check in with my clients and my free agents to make sure things are running smoothly in my absence.

REASON #5: And yes, I am well on my way to achieving financial independence.

Notice, however, that financial independence is not mentioned until my *fifth* priority. That's not to say that money isn't important to me. I want to make money because of the personal freedom and security that it provides. But financial wealth is not my end goal.

For those who list financial wealth as their number one goal, the journey is often much harder. These people might say, "I want to make $10 million and retire by age fifty; I don't care how I make the money, I just want to make it." They then spend twenty to thirty years toiling and slaving to make that money. Very often, they burn out or sometimes even work themselves to death before they can enjoy the fruits of their labors. When they do reach that coveted sum and are able to retire, many times they look around and say to themselves, "Okay, I've got all this money, but I have no idea how to use it to enjoy life as I've always wanted to."

I personally think it is better to work for a more modest but steady income doing work that I enjoy and believe in, than to spend years working for a targeted sum of $X million that I may never reach. I want to enjoy the *quality of my journey* through life. I have done this by achieving my first reason, my desire to build a good communications company. The money has come only as a *result* of achieving this first goal.

I can't tell you how good it feels to be on the road to achieving most of my business and personal goals. I know that much of what I've accomplished has come with the help and counsel of numerous other people. (Please see the list of people who have influenced my life and helped me in my business ventures at the beginning of this book.) I also realize that it could all end tomorrow. I certainly hope not, but it could. But that's all the more reason for me to keep working towards my goals. Since my business provides me with the quality of life that I enjoy, I will enjoy my life while it lasts.

Having owned my own business for over fifteen years, I now wouldn't trade it for anything. I would find it difficult, if not impossible, to go back to the 8 AM to 5 PM routine. It's not that I can't work for anyone but myself. When you are self-employed, you often work for many people at once. Like a politician, you sometimes have more "bosses" than you did when you worked for a regular company. But having owned my own business, I would now have a very hard time going back to work in the daily structure of corporate business, a structure that I think is wasteful and outdated.

WHAT ARE *YOUR* REASONS?

When hard times come, it's important to have good reasons for putting yourself through the grind of sustaining your own business. It's not enough just to say, "I have my own reasons for being self-employed." You have to *feel* those reasons and *believe in them* in order to reaffirm your efforts. If you can't think of at least five good reasons why you want to be self-employed, it will be better to stick with your day job.

Again, the most essential question to ask yourself is *why* you want to start your own business in the first place? Is it money? Is it independence? Or do you have an incredible concept that you want to launch and turn into a business?

What are your reasons?

a._____

b._____

c._____

d._____

e._____

CHAPTER TWO

———⟫●⟨———

The Parable of Lake Destination

When you are self-employed, it will be impossible to separate your business from your lifestyle. This is not as ominous as it sounds. One of your major goals, above all, should be to enjoy the quality of your journey, not necessarily the destination. That is the ultimate lifestyle decision. The way you view the world (that is, your **mindset**) and the way you structure your **lifestyle** are all within your own grasp.

To see what your journey will be like as a self-employed business owner, let's look at a parable. Since I am in the communication business, I often use analogies to make important points. This one examines the path you will take and the lifestyle choices you must make when you decide to start your own business.

Let's say you are a recreational hiker whose experience has thus far been limited to one-day hikes on sunny days. You decide you want to try longer, more serious hikes that might take up to a week to complete. In particular, there is one place that you've always wanted to visit. It's called Lake Destination. You've never been there before, but you've seen pictures of it in a hiking book and it looks gorgeous. It is a beautiful alpine lake located far in the mountains, surrounded on all sides by snow-capped peaks and beautiful evergreen forests.

You have always wanted to take this hike, but you've been putting it off for some time because (a.) you were always too busy, (b.) the weather was bad, (c.) you couldn't find anyone to go with you, etc. Some of your reasons for postponing this hike were valid, but lately they have started to seem like excuses for not going ahead and doing it.

Then one morning, at the start of your annual two-week vacation, you look in the mirror and say, "Today I begin my journey to Lake Destination." You call around to see if any of your friends would like to join you, but no one is available. The hike will be a bit more tedious and lonely all by yourself. But no matter! You've finally decided to make the hike. So you pack up your gear and hit the road.

After a two-hour drive, you come to the trailhead. Actually, you discover that there are *two* different trails leading to Lake Destination. Each trail has a sign marked with the distance to the lake. One trail is five miles long; the other is twenty miles long. The five-mile trail would be the obvious choice here. It is shorter in length and will get you to your destination faster. But to be safe, you check your hiking guide, which has a map of the two trails.

According to the guide, the five-mile trail is indeed the faster route. It will take about ten hours, the book says, for the average hiker to reach Lake Destination. But as you read on, you learn that the five-mile trail is rather dangerous, with steep grades and switchbacks. The guidebook warns you to be very careful hiking this trail, since it is not very well maintained or monitored. If you fall and break your ankle on this trail, it will be very difficult for someone to rescue you. The guidebook also says that the scenery on the five-mile trail is not very spectacular. Furthermore, the five-mile trail "dead-ends" in an area on the lake shore where the campsites are surrounded by thick woods. There are no other trails out of this area, so once you reach the lake, you won't be able to hike in any other direction.

Still, you favor taking the five-mile trail, since it will get you to Lake Destination faster. Like most of us, you are always searching for the fastest route from Point A to Point B. All your life, you've been taught that speed is king, and that the quicker you get to your destination, or the faster you accomplish a project, the better you will be judged.

But just to be sure, you read about the twenty-mile trail. Again your instincts are correct. According to the guidebook, the twenty-mile hike will take up to three days. The twenty-mile trail is very well-maintained, with smooth paths and very gradual grade increases. Furthermore, this path is blessed with incredible scenery: waterfalls, snow-capped mountains, wild rivers, amazing wildlife, and outstanding camping facilities along the way. Because of the camping facilities, the twenty-mile trail is thoroughly monitored, so if you get into trouble, you can easily find help.

You also find out that at the end of the twenty-mile trail, when you have reached Lake Destination, there are plenty of opportunities for hikes to other beautiful lakes. There is Lake Independence, also Lake Freedom and Lake Flexibility. The hiking book tells you that these lakes are actually more beautiful than Lake Destination.

Now you have a problem. What you thought was an obvious choice is suddenly not so obvious. Old habits die hard, so you still favor the five-mile option. But then you remember that you have a full two weeks vacation to make this hike—so, in fact, either trail will work. If you take the twenty-mile trail and it takes you three days to get to Lake Destination, you will still have eight to ten days to hike to the other lakes and come back again. Now the thought of hiking the five-mile trail, a short and dangerous trail that leads to a dead end, isn't so appealing. So, you ask yourself, what's the rush? The more you think about it, the more you like the idea of the twenty-mile trail, with its beautiful vistas and campsites along the hike.

Which choice will you make? In the end, it's really up to you, your values, and your mindset as a hiker.

By now, you're probably *counting* the analogies in this story! This book is clearly about taking the twenty-mile trail to Lake Destination, the lake itself being a metaphor for retirement. The five-mile trail to the lake is about speed, greater risks, and coming to an absolute end. The twenty-mile trail is about enjoying the quality of life that you experience on the journey, rather than trying to get from here to there as quickly as possible.

Which is more important to you? Reaching the destination as soon as possible or enjoying the quality of life on the journey?

Deciding to take the hike to Lake Destination is analogous to finally deciding to start your own business. As with taking the hike, you have probably thought about going into business for yourself many times. Then one day you decide to take the plunge. Going on the hike alone is like going into business solo. It might be preferable for you to have someone along to share the experiences. But if you are really serious about being self-employed, it will be much better if you make the journey alone.

The crucial question you must ask yourself before you become self-employed is: Which is more important to you? Reaching the destination as soon as possible or enjoying the quality of life on the journey? If the destination, which is analogous to making quick money, is more important, then self-employment is probably not for you. If your major goal in life is not to retire but to seek new challenges and hike to new destinations, read on!

Another story that explains different scenarios on how to achieve a goal is the story of the tortoise and the hare. At the beginning of the race, the hare was blazing off the starting line. The tortoise was slow but very steady. The hare burned out early, fell asleep halfway through the race, and couldn't make it to the finish line. The tortoise took a long time to finish, but eventually won the race. A tortoise's pace may be a little slow for my personal tastes, but I hope you get the point. Slow and steady is better.

CHAPTER THREE

The Self-Employed Business Mindset

The concepts featured in this book for starting a successful business are centered on two basic beliefs:

1. We are the sum total of our **Mindset**.

2. Our present and future **Lifestyle** evolves from this Mindset.

What do I mean by "mindset?" Well, your mindset is simply the way you think and feel about things in general. Our mindset is the sum total of our *emotional* and *personality traits*. It is formed from *experiences* and *behaviors* learned during the course of our lifetime. In this case, we are actually dealing with *two mindsets*. There is your *personal mindset*—that is, the way you think and feel about the world and your everyday life. And then there is your *business mindset*—that is, the way you think and feel about your own personal business and the work that you do at your job.

Your *business mindset* is an extension of your *personal mindset*. Like most people, you develop attitudes and opinions about work and employment through the work that you do. If you have occasionally changed jobs, or even changed careers, you know that your business mindset changes as your employment changes. You develop new attitudes and new opinions—some positive, some negative—as you sample new jobs and new types of employment. Our goal here is to see if your personal and business mindsets will fit well into the *self-employed business mindset*—that is, the mindset of a self-employed business owner.

If you have the right *emotional* and *personality traits*, it will be very easy to put yourself in the business mindset for self-employment. These traits will be the most important factors in making your business succeed over the long term. Again, this book is meant to help you to identify these traits. (If you have some, but not all, of these personality traits, don't worry. You can still take advantage of the traits that you have and work on developing the ones that you don't have.)

I once read an article about the things a person should do if they were preparing to run for political office. A good part of this article dealt with the technical side of running a political campaign. It offered tips on such things as how to select a campaign manager, how to form a campaign committee, how to advertise your campaign using newspapers, direct mail, TV and radio, etc. But this article also spoke effectively about the emotional and personal characteristics that it takes to be a successful political candidate. The article asked questions of the soul and talked about what the potential politician should consider before they even file for office. The questions included:

1. How do you react to criticism? Are you thin-skinned?

2. Is it easy for you to ask people for favors?

3. Are you comfortable asking people for money?

4. Do you enjoy being around people?

5. Can you keep up with the rigorous schedule that a campaign requires?

6. Is running for political office worth the disruption to your home life?

7. How are you getting along with your spouse? Can your marriage handle the strain of a political campaign? What is your relationship with your children?

8. Is your family supportive of your efforts? Do they understand what you are about to do and why? Are they willing to make the necessary sacrifices that it will take for you to run a successful campaign?

These are the kinds of questions that a person should ask before they make the major life-changing commitment of running for political office. Ironically, these kinds of questions are often overlooked by the potential office seeker.

I have developed my own set of questions along these lines for those who are thinking of starting their own business. What follows is a quick test of personal questions that examine the *emotional* and *personality traits* of a potential small business owner. We will be examining these traits, and how they apply to the self-employed business mindset, throughout this book.

This test will help you to determine your prospects for success as an entrepreneur and whether or not your personal mindset is a good match for the mindset of a small business owner. (Questions about your potential *lifestyle* as a self-employed business owner, which are just as important, will be asked in the next chapter.)

THE TEST

This test is very simple. Read the questions below and assign yourself a number between 1 and 5, where 1 is the lowest score, and 5 is the highest. For example, in the first question—"Are you a leader?"—a score of 1 means "I have absolutely no leadership skills whatsoever. My dog doesn't even follow me on walks." A score of 5 means "I am an experienced leader in every sense of the word. If not for my dream of starting my own business, I would be running for president."

My only precaution here is: **Be completely honest with yourself on this test!** Do not make yourself out to be more (or less) than you really are. Again, this test will help you to determine your prospects for success, but *only* if you are honest in assessing your own strengths and weaknesses.

_____ Are you a leader?

_____ Are you a confident person?

_____ When faced with a difference of opinion, are you able to see the other person's point of view, even if you don't agree with it?

_____ Do you have a good deal of patience, even when things don't always go your way?

_____ Can you make decisions easily?

_____ Do you mind working alone?

_____ Do you have a strong sense of pride in your work?

_____ Do you execute your tasks easily?

_____ Can you handle failure?

_____ Can you handle success?

_____ Are you creative?

_____ Do you consider yourself to be a social person?

_____ Do you trust people and enjoy being around them?

_____ Are you organized?

_____ Do you have a good sense of humor?

_____ Do you have the ability to focus on small details while still keeping the "big picture" in mind?

_____ Do you exercise good judgment?

_____ Are you able to work effectively under pressure?

_____ Are you well-liked and respected by the people you work with?

_____ Are you comfortable selling your product or service?

_____ Do you consider yourself to be ethical and a person of integrity?

_____ Can you handle multiple tasks at once?

_____ Are you a flexible person?

_____ Do you use your time wisely?

_____ Are you good with finances?

GRADING THE TEST

OK, class, it's time for the answers.

- **120-125 Points.** You obviously didn't read the paragraph before the start of the test, asking you to be completely honest. You are not very reflective and have an ego the size of Mount Everest. I would advise visiting a psychiatrist before you consider starting a business.

- **100-119 Points:** Your prospects for success are outstanding. You are very good to excellent in the crucial areas of what it takes to sustain a business. What are you waiting for? Call me when you get your business to a sustainable level, which shouldn't take long. I'd like to work with you.

- **88-99 Points:** Your prospects are good to very good. Go through the test again and pick out the traits where you scored lower and then honestly evaluate whether you feel that you can improve in those areas.

- **75-87 Points:** You have scored an average for all of the combined traits for measuring your prospects for success. Unless you improve in many areas you will have an average chance of succeeding.

- **Below 74 Points:** Self-employment is not for you. You really do not have the critical personality traits or the right temperament to sustain a business over an extended period of time.

MY OWN GRADE

Just to let you know that I myself am *NOT* necessarily the "very model" of a modern major self-employed business owner, I took my own test and scored a 99. That's a little lower than I would have hoped for, but my prospects for continuing success are at the high end of "good to very good."

I scored lower with respect to handling failure and adversity and being able to work well under pressure. I also scored lower in the area of sales; I am a good salesman, but not a great one. I could also stand to be a little less sensitive, more patient, and not quite as emotional when things don't go my way. A top salesman looks at a closed door as just another opportunity to open up the next door. They view rejection as a learning experience. The only question an "A" businessperson has is "What can I do to be more effective next time?"

I scored very well in the areas of execution, judgment, decision-making, flexibility, organization, finances, and integrity.

So now that you've taken the test, you have some idea of your own strengths and weaknesses, and whether or not you might be suitable for self-employment. If you'd like to know more about the mindset of being a small business owner, by all means, keep reading. Even if, after taking this test, you have already decided that self-employment is *not* for you, I still encourage you to read on. Again, I will be examining the emotional and personality traits that are measured in this self-test in detail throughout this book. These traits can help you in your job performance no matter what type of job you have, and taking an in-depth look at these traits may help you to find new ways of using and developing them to your advantage.

THE FREE AGENCY PERSPECTIVE

As a self-employed business owner, I operate under what I call *the free agency perspective*. Being a free agent basically means that you are in business for yourself, even if you happen to work for other people. It means that you are always trying to do your best possible work on your current job or project, and that you are always looking for your *next* job or project as well. You are in the service of many, but your loyalty and devotion are to yourself and your family.

By the power invested in me, I hereby declare you a *"free agent."* You are now: **Your Name Inc.** So write down your first and last name on this line:

_____INC.

"Free agency" is not just another catch-phrase to describe the entrepreneurial spirit. The self-employed free agent is like the undercover agent of the business world, working for several clients at once instead of one single employer. These clients can include everyone from individual customers to small and medium-sized businesses to billion-dollar corporations.

Self-employed free agents have the freedom to conduct their business anytime, anywhere, often beneath the clumsy and predictable radar of Big Business. They are not hampered by the outdated business models, lack of effective communication, and slow decision-making processes that often plague large companies. In fact, the corporate disadvantages that slow the progress of Big Business often work to the advantage of self-employed free agents. Many large companies will pay self-employed free agents to perform specialized tasks that they themselves cannot handle. Self-employed free agents are comfortable in the age of rapid information exchange, and can conduct business with a speed and efficiency that is often not possible in large companies.

The self-employed free agent often works with other free agents. My own company has no employees, but at any give time I employ up to seventeen part-time people of various wide-ranging skills to handle the needs of my clients. I refer to these people as *"free agents,"* never as "contractors" or "consultants."

Competition among self-employed free agents is varied and stimulating. It fosters a creative process and fair market trade that recalls a more meaningful time, when one person's ideas often became a reality. This is no dream or wishful thinking; it is a practical and very real way to do business. My free agency perspective has helped me to sustain a successful, independent business for over fifteen years.

CORPORATE EMPLOYMENT AND THE FREE AGENCY PERSPECTIVE

The best thing about the free agency perspective is *you don't have to be self-employed to adopt it.* You can think of yourself a "free agent" even if you work for a mega-conglomerate, a corporation, or a small business, are in government service, or are unemployed. In fact, even if you ultimately decide *not* to start your own business and to stick with a full-time job, it's still a good idea to adopt the free-agent mentality.

It used to be that people would work for one company all their lives. They would be hired by that company just out of high school or college and would work there until they retired. But job security is fast becoming a thing of the past. Companies regularly lay off employees and eliminate jobs to cut costs and to keep their stockholders happy. It is probable that you will make five or six job or career changes during your lifetime. This may not be fair, but if you *accept* that this is the way things are, it becomes easier to see yourself in the free-agent mentality.

At the moment, you may be lending your expertise to Acme, Inc., and be compensated for your work. As long as this arrangement remains mutually beneficial, your relationship will continue. Always give your best effort to the projects that you handle for your current employer. Remember, you will always be judged by the success or failure of your most recent work.

As you work on each job or project, always be on the lookout for your "next gig." If you find a new project within your company, take it. If you look ahead and don't see a new project developing with that company, or if you see hard times and possible layoffs on the horizon, it might be a good idea to start looking around at new companies with new projects that might need your talents more.

Even if you never start your own business, adopting the free agency perspective will give you an advantage. As a free agent, you assume the responsibility for your own success and well-being. If you accept the fact that nothing is permanent in today's job market, it becomes easier to anticipate and prepare for the transition points in your career. You will no longer see your long-term success as being dependent on your current employer. You will see *yourself* as the ultimate master of your own destiny.

FREE AGENCY: BASEBALL HOLDS THE KEY

The concept of being a free agent is nothing new. Major League Baseball introduced free agency in the 1970's. A player no longer plays for the San Francisco Giants, the Cleveland Indians, or the New York Yankees. The baseball player now lends his talents to a baseball team for a certain agreed-upon period of time. When that time expires, the player bids his talents to the next-highest bidder. I now look at a player like Jason Giambi as Jason Giambi, Inc. He lent his talents to the Oakland A's for several years until a better deal came along, and he moved to the New York Yankees.

The entertainment industry is also loaded with free agents. In Hollywood's Golden Age, actors like Humphrey Bogart, Bette Davis, and Jimmy Stewart were "under contract" with a certain movie studio, such as Paramount or Universal, to appear in a certain number of films for that studio per year. Now, stars like Julia Roberts, Jim Carrey, Scarlett Johansson, and Tom Hanks work for different studios, and negotiate each movie deal separately.

> **Always look at yourself as free agent. It's a mindset that you must have if you wish to start a successful business.**

Always look at yourself as free agent. It's a mindset that you must have if you wish to start a successful business. If you are working with a company, view yourself as a free agent who is lending your expertise to that company for a period of time. You are Steve Jackson, Inc., or Pamela Olsen, Inc.

INNOVATOR VS. FOLLOWER

When it comes to starting your own business, there are two kinds of entrepreneurs: The Innovator and the Follower. The Innovator is one who tries to sell a new concept or a new way of doing business. Bill Gates is an example of an Innovator. Thirty years ago, almost no one had a computer, much less computer software, in their house or office. Bill Gates and his contemporaries invented software that could be used by everyday people with no training at all in computer programming. Another innovator of our time is Jeff Bezos. Fifteen years ago, the Internet was just starting to come into widespread use and was then used mostly for e-mail and business transactions. With Amazon.com, Jeff Bezos introduced a new concept—that something (in this case, books) could be *sold* to everyday consumers over the Internet.

A Follower is an entrepreneur who follows a tried-and-true, tested product or service, like a home-cleaning business, landscaping, or a plumbing enterprise. The foundation has already been established for this type of business, and the entrepreneur's major goal is to find their own niche. These types of businesses may not be sexy, but they typically succeed more than those of the Innovators. The Follower doesn't have to work as hard as the Innovator to establish the *need* for their product or service in the minds of their clients or customers. The potential client already knows the benefits of a home-cleaning or landscaping service, or of calling in a plumber to fix the sink.

Whether you are an Innovator or a Follower, but especially if you are an Innovator, the self-employed business mindset is a necessity. An Innovator faces the daunting task of trying to convince clients or customers that they need this new product or service, even though they have never tried it before. It takes time to convince people to try something new, and to establish it in their minds so that they keep coming back to it. During this time, you've got to keep yourself in business, and that means using your time well and handling your finances responsibly as you seek out new clients, test and improve your product or service, and develop your customer base.

If you are a Follower, you don't face the struggle of introducing something new to your potential clients, but you still have the task of convincing them that they should do business with *you*. Even if they have used your type of product or service before, they will be more likely to do business with a well-established company than with a free agent who is just starting out. It may take a while for you to locate the clients in your area who need your *exact* product or service. Or you may find that you have to make adjustments to your business, because the demand for your product or service is not as strong as you thought it would be.

FOLLOW YOUR PASSION: YES...

As I said before, I believe in half the statement, "Follow your passion, and the money will follow." Of course you should find something that you are passionate about if your goal is to be in business for an extended period of time. But again, to suggest that being passionate will automatically lead to success is simply not true.

When I first started my business in 1988, I was not selling radio air time for advertising, as I am now. I published a small-press newspaper aimed at the aging population. I had previously served as Executive Director of the Puget Sound chapter of the Altzheimer's Association and saw a need for this type of publication. However, over time I discovered that I didn't have the same passion that some of my fellow small-press colleagues had in publishing their newspapers. I was proud every time a newspaper came off the press, but my heart wasn't entirely in it.

I had been in the newspaper business for five years and was still struggling. I gradually realized that a publication was the wrong venue to reach my target audience. Many of the topics I was covering in my newspaper—travel, financial planning, hobbies such as golf—were not specific to the aging population. I started to look around for a new means of communicating with my older audience, while at the same time providing advertising for the clients who had supported my newspaper.

I have always had a passion for radio and broadcasting, ever since I was a kid living in New York, listening to Yankees games on a transistor radio in my room at night. I inherited a deep voice from my grandfather, and many times when I went into a grocery store or a restaurant, people asked me if I was on the radio. When I answered "No," they often said, "You should be."

I approached a local independent radio station that catered to an older audience with the idea of hosting a weekly radio show that would explore current events and topics of interest to their listeners. Using a system called "block programming," where radio time is sold for half-hour or one-hour periods, usually on Saturday and Sunday mornings, for radio shows and "infomercials," I purchased thirty minutes of airtime each week and produced and hosted my own show, featuring the clients that were advertising in my newspaper over the broadcast waves.

At first, I saw this option as a supplement to my publication. In addition to advertising space in my newspaper, I could now offer my clients broadcast time on the radio. It gave me a competitive advantage over the other newspapers targeting the older demographic. But the show worked so well that I eventually phased out the publication and completely devoted my energies to radio. This provided me with a good living and positioned me for the next opportunity that came along.

...THE MONEY WILL FOLLOW: MAYBE

We have all heard stories about the single mother with eight children on welfare who started a day-care center and is now a multimillionaire living on Park Avenue. You know the story because it's the type of story that would be covered on Oprah. The *reason* it is covered on Oprah in the first place is because it *is* such an unusual and rare story.

I repeat: Just *because you are a great artist, it doesn't mean that you can run an art gallery.* Just because your friends say you are a great cook, it doesn't mean that you can run a successful restaurant.

Although you may be passionate about your business in the beginning, your passion will soon begin to wear off when you deal with the realities of running a business. When I first started my weekly radio show, I really enjoyed the work. But after a while, it became like any other business. It's all about meeting deadlines and making sure that your bank account is operating in the black.

I don't want to diminish your need or desire to do something that you enjoy. Goals and missions are very critical ingredients to long-range success. This can make the difference in being able to sustain a business for life. But again, *never confuse the dream with the reality.*

If, for example, your dream is to open an art gallery, the reality will be choosing a good location, advertising in local newspapers and magazines, hosting promotional events to showcase new artists, making contacts within the local and national art communities, and showing up for work every day to earn enough to pay your rent and utilities. If your dream is to open an accounting or marketing service, the reality will be making cold calls every day to potential clients, advertising your services through direct mail, attending local chamber of commerce meetings, paying your bills, and providing your clients with exceptional service that meets or exceeds their expectations. *These are the factors that will determine the success or failure of your business.*

> **Never confuse the dream with the reality.**

As for my radio show, it made money, but never as much as I would have liked. I decided to put the show on hiatus when a better opportunity came along. As part of my show, I had been buying radio air time for my newspaper advertising clients. I received a call from the sales manager of a software company, who asked me to purchase air time for their own radio commercials. Soon, I was doing media buying for other companies who had not been connected with my newspaper or my radio show. Rather than running on one local station, I was now planning, creating, producing, and distributing radio commercials all over the United States. The prospects for professional and financial rewards were enormous. I was able to stay in radio, but in a more successful venture than my radio show had been. The "money followed, " but not in the way I had expected.

WANT A QUICK BUCK? GO TO LAS VEGAS!

In a world where there is no longer any such thing as a traditional career path, where five or six career changes in one lifetime has become the norm for many people, starting your own business may be the best way to achieve security for yourself and your family. But be aware, *it will take time!* You cannot expect to establish security as a self-employed business owner overnight.

Starting a successful business is not about making the quick buck. Actually, making fast money is contrary to starting a long-term, successful business. It goes against building relationships with your clients and competitors, and tinkering with your concept over an extended period of time. The more money you risk trying to get rich quick, the more money you can lose.

The only people who get rich selling videos and books with this "quick-wealth" approach are the people hawking the schemes.

Yesterday, I heard a radio commercial from an individual who was selling a book and CD on how you can get rich in the real estate market. He claimed that there was absolutely no risk involved and that you would be wealthy within one year. The word "R-I-C-H" was even part of the phone number that you were to call to obtain this magical money-making formula. Whether it's real estate, a can't-miss direct marketing scheme, or a video that will make you an overnight positive thinker, we are deluged with infomercials, books, and CDs telling us how we can reverse our misfortunes instantly. I strongly urge you to resist these get-rich temptations. Your odds for instant wealth are higher in Las Vegas. The only people who get rich selling videos and books with this "quick-wealth" approach are the people hawking the schemes.

The mindset of the self-employed business owner should not be geared toward making fast money. It should be geared toward establishing a long-term business that will provide security for you and your family in good times and bad. It may take several (e.g., three to five) years, depending on your product or service, to build your business and make it profitable. But once you establish that business, it may be profitable enough to provide you with better financial security than any job you've had before.

A WORD ABOUT BUSINESS PLANS

As I mentioned in the Introduction, this book does not offer much business theory. Many business books on the market today are written by corporate business people, or by academic people who have never actually run a small business. Often, these books deal with the theory and structure of starting a business, but tell you nothing about the everyday decisions and the problems that you will face as a business owner. Most of these books have one thing in common: They all spend a great deal of time discussing the need for a business plan.

While I think it is important to have a business plan, I also believe that too much is made of it by business gurus. Again, this is not to say that business plans are useless. Writing a plan for your business can give you some sense of what you want to accomplish and where you want your business to be in a year or in five years. But I strongly recommend that you don't become a slave to your business plan. Many times, business plans keep you from doing what you *should* be doing. I have talked with numerous people who were thinking of starting their own business, but who never get past the "business plan" stage.

I recently heard from a friend who lost his regular job: "I want to start my own private practice as an architect." I think my friend would have a very good chance of starting a successful business. He has plenty of experience and also has many of the emotional and personality traits necessary for a self-employed business owner that I discuss in this book. But my friend absolutely *refuses* to start his practice without a long-range business plan. He is such a slave to continuous planning that he cannot start a business without first mapping out a long-term strategy for himself. And yet, he never seems to be able to sit down and write out a business plan. He is avoiding what he feels is a crucial step to starting his own business.

My response to him would be "The hell with the business plan! You need clients for your architecture practice! Get on the phone and start making it happen! Everything else will take care of itself!" But I'm betting that my friend will not go into business for himself at this time, even though he is in a perfect position to do so. He will go out and find a new permanent position that he hopes will be more secure than his last job.

The mindset of the self-employed business owner requires *flexibility* and a willingness to change tactics when things don't go your way. Business plans have a tendency to become outdated very quickly. For example, after six months in business, you may discover that you should be seeking out a different kind of clientele, or that your marketing plan is flawed and needs to be reworked. It is better to change your goals and adjust your strategies than to stubbornly adhere to a business plan that is not working out. If I've learned anything as a self-employed business owner, it's that there is no one "right way" to start a successful business.

A WARNING AGAINST PREJUDICES

One final word about the self-employed business mindset (and this applies to almost any mindset). You will go a lot farther, in this world and in business, if you have an open mind. As human beings, we all develop prejudices or preconceived ideas about events and other people. But your chances of success in business will be much higher if you leave your prejudices at the door.

I say this not just for the sake of morality but from a practical point of view. In the future, business will be conducted more and more by diverse groups of people from many different backgrounds, ethnic groups, races, religions, nationalities, etc. If you believe that people have much more in common than less in common, and if you embrace rather than isolate, your prospects for success will be that much better. What's more, you will have a huge advantage over your competition if they believe otherwise.

CHAPTER FOUR

The Self-Employed Lifestyle

As with the questions concerning the emotional and personality traits that make up your business mindset, there are essential questions that you must ask yourself about your own personal lifestyle. As I said before, there is no easy road to wealth when you are self-employed. During the early years, when your business is just starting out, you will not have much money to spend, and a good part of the money you do earn will go back into helping you to develop your business. It is important not only that *you* should understand this, but also that *your spouse* and *your family* should understand this as well.

The following are examples of the kinds of "lifestyle questions" that future entrepreneurs must ask of themselves *and* their family before starting their own business:

1. Since going into business for yourself is a major lifestyle choice, if you are married, does your spouse understand and support what you are about to do?

2. Does your spouse realize that your primary focus in life for the foreseeable future (e.g., three to five years) will be your business?

3.   If your spouse has a job, do they understand that there may be times in the next three to five years when they may be the "sole breadwinner" for the family? Are they willing to support the family financially during the time when you are building your business?

4.   Are you and your spouse both flexible people? Can you roll with the punches and setbacks that starting your own business will inevitably bring?

5.   Do family members realize that they may have to live more frugally for the next couple of years? Are they prepared to trade in the SUV for a used car? Maybe you will have to downsize and move into a less expensive house.

6.   Will your kids be satisfied wearing $35 tennis shoes rather than the $150 brand types?

7.   Do you or your family members need the security of a regular paycheck?

INSTANT GRATIFICATION

There has never been a better time in history to go into business for yourself than right now. At the dawn of the 21st century, we have resources available to help us start a business that our parents and grandparents never dreamed of. Unprecedented technology, financing, education, health, personal wealth, knowledge, and mobility are all at a higher level than ever before.

But there is a downside to all these advantages. We have created a culture of Instant Gratification, in which we feel we must have everything "right here, right now!" We live in one of the wealthiest countries on

We have created a culture of Instant Gratification, in which we feel we must have everything "right here, right now!"

Earth, and most Americans have a pretty easy life. At times, it seems as if our lives are ruled by speed. This is a culture of instant customer service, overnight shipping, twenty-four-hour ATM machines, thirty-minute oil change and lube jobs, self-service gas pumps, and one-stop shopping. We can eat lunch every day at fast-food restaurants, and for dinner at home, we pop a frozen entrée in the microwave and cook it in five minutes. We can travel to anywhere in the world in a matter of hours, not days or weeks, as it was with our ancestors.

Thanks to the technological innovations of the past forty years, almost anything we could ever need is now a remote control button or mouse-click away. We can order books, clothes, appliances, music, movie tickets, plane reservations, and even food on the Internet, and we can find information about any company in the world by accessing its web page. We can send instant e-mails to relatives across the country and to business associates around the world. With cellular phones, we can call anyone anywhere at any time *from* anywhere at any time. We have created a world where it seems there should be no reason to have to wait for *anything*.

(Some people have even become impatient with Instant Gratification itself. As Carrie Fisher jokingly complains in her book *Postcards From the Edge*, "Instant gratification takes too long!")

Even business itself seems to be conducted at light speed. Thanks to the Internet and twenty-four-hour cable news services, stock prices and market results are now reported *minute by minute*, not day by day. At 10 AM, the Dow Jones is up, the NASDAQ is down. At 11:35 AM, the Dow is even, the NASDAQ is up. At 2:15 PM, the Dow is down, the NASDAQ is even. At 4 PM, the markets close down.

Also in this Information Age, companies seem to start up quicker and gain high-profile status much more easily. Ten years ago, when the Internet was just starting to become available to the general public, companies like Amazon.com, Yahoo, E-Bay, and

Google didn't even exist. If Jeff Bezos can create a business out of his garage using nothing but his computer, and four years later become *Time* magazine's Person of the Year for his contribution to the "New Economy," then surely we, the self-employed entrepreneur, should be able to achieve similar success in roughly the same amount of time. Or so we think!

It is good to remember that even the most successful "New Economy" companies have had a rocky start, all appearances to the contrary. Amazon.com, Yahoo, and Google have all survived the economic downturn of recent years, but not without laying off a good part of their workforce. All three of these companies have only recently started to turn profits. It is also good to remember that for every successful dot-com start-up in any category (search engines, online trade, consumer goods), there are a dozen more like it that have gone out of business or have been bought out by larger companies. (See my case study of the failure of HomeGrocer/Webvan later in this book for an in-depth analysis of how *not* to start a business.)

NEWS FLASH: THERE IS NO SILVER BULLET

Instant gratification and starting your own business do not mix. Again, it takes *time* (typically three to five years) to build a sustainable business. And during that time, you must live frugally, save as much money as you can, and keep out of as much debt as possible. It will

> **Instant Gratification and starting your own business do not mix.**

serve you and your business well if you can replace the creed of Instant Gratification in your mind with an ethic of sensible decision-making.

I believe one of the biggest reasons why most people don't go into business for themselves is that they are unwilling to make the necessary sacrifices to make it happen. When you talk to would-be entrepreneurs, they say all the right things about wanting to start their own business. But when you probe further, many times you find out that what is *really* important to them is having the five-bedroom house with a three-car garage and a brand new SUV. In other words, they define their success by their material possessions, by how much money they can make in the shortest amount of time, not by the kind of business they would like to start and whether or not they can sustain it over the long run.

We must make choices in our lives. If you want a top-paying corporate job, you might have to surrender control of your time. You will give up some independence, and perhaps some freedom of thought and association. In exchange, you will acquire a nice house in a nice neighborhood and plenty of fun toys. Again, *there is nothing wrong with this kind of life*. If that is your choice of how you want to live, I wish you well. There is something positive to be said for someone else signing your paycheck.

> **Your business will always come first. It will be the primary motivation behind most, if not all, of your major lifestyle decisions.**

But if you really have the desire to start your own business, it can be done. And yes, if your business does well, it is possible to eventually earn that five-bedroom house with the three-car garage and the SUV if you really want them. But it will take time and sacrifice on your part. Understand that when you are a self-employed business owner, your business will always come first. It will be the primary motivation behind most, if not all, of your major lifestyle decisions. Bottom line: There is no silver bullet.

YOUR PERSONAL LIFESTYLE

What kind of lifestyle are you looking for? No one can answer that question but you. As I said at the beginning of the previous chapter, your lifestyle is defined by your mindset. Just as you have both a personal and a business mindset, you will also have both a *personal* and a *business lifestyle*. As a self-employed business owner, you will sometimes find it hard to separate the two. Your business lifestyle will greatly influence your personal lifestyle, and vice versa.

For a good time after you start your own business, your personal lifestyle will be largely governed by your business mindset. You must make personal lifestyle decisions based on how well your business is doing, how much income you have, and how that income will be divided between business and personal necessities. The bottom line is, your chances of success as a self-employed business owner will be much greater if you can find contentment without acquiring all the material trappings for an extended period of time.

I am always impressed with the Koreans, Vietnamese, and other immigrants who come to this "land of opportunity." They are willing to make the necessary sacrifices in order to build and sustain their own businesses. Many times a Vietnamese family will live in rooms above their small grocery store or restaurant to save money. Often, they have never been to college or taken a business class, but they instinctively know that it is essential to keep your *overhead costs low* to keep a business going.

In your own case, the extent to which having your own business will affect your personal lifestyle depends on a variety of factors: What type of business you start, your personal circumstances (e.g., Are you married or single? Do you have children? Does your spouse work? Do you live in a house or an apartment? etc.), and how successful—or unsuccessful—your business is over the years. The point is that you must be flexible enough to adjust your personal lifestyle so that it fits within the means of your business.

If you have a family, it is important that they understand what you are doing and why you want to start your own business. It is also important that they understand how this will affect *their* lives as well as yours. Before you start your business, sit down with your family and make sure everyone understands the ways in which this may affect them. For example, money for personal items, such as toys and clothes, may be limited for a time. The family may not be able to take big vacations for a few years. As a business owner, you may not be available at times for family activities, or to serve family needs (e.g., taking the kids to soccer practice), because your business will take precedent.

Hopefully, the adjustments that you and your family will have to make to your personal lives will be minimal. But be aware that there may come a time, even after you have established your business, when you will have to make a significant change in your personal lifestyle to keep your business afloat.

But the more flexible you can be in adjusting your personal lifestyle to suit your business, the more that lifestyle will be an asset to you, instead of a burden.

About ten years ago, when I was still publishing my newspaper, one of my advertising clients, a retirement center, suddenly went bankrupt. I had just completed a major printing job for this client. As part of my agreement with the printers who had handled the job, I had promised to pay them once the client paid me. When the client went out of business, I got stuck with a printing bill for $10,000. To keep my business from going under, I had to move out of my four-bedroom house and into a condo that I had originally leased to use as office space. This move saved me about $38,000 a year, and enabled me to pay off my debt to the printers. I'm glad to report that I have since been able to move back into a four-bedroom house.

What happened to me was an extreme case. I was single at the time, so changing my address, while certainly a great inconvenience, was easier for me than it would have been if I had been married with a family. Hopefully, you will never be forced to give up your house to save your business. But the more flexible you can be in adjusting your personal lifestyle to suit your business, the more that lifestyle will be an asset to you instead of a burden.

YOUR BUSINESS LIFESTYLE

The kind of business lifestyle you lead when you are self-employed will depend on the kind of business you start. Again, your lifestyle evolves from your mindset. We will be examining the elements of the self-employed business mindset, and the different ways that these elements will affect your business lifestyle throughout this book.

The business lifestyle is different for every self-employed business owner, and it changes over time as your business progresses. When I first started my business, I spent most of my days making sales calls to potential advertisers for my newspaper, and later to potential clients for my media buying service. Now, most of my new clients come to me through referrals from other clients. I am in the position of being sold to, not of selling. I spend my work days creating radio campaigns for my clients, meeting with free agents to handle the development of those campaigns, and paying bills and invoices.

In general, the more routine and boring your work days become, the more successful your business will be.

If you work hard at establishing your business, and continuously offer a quality product or service, eventually you will reach the point where potential clients are seeking you out instead of the other way around. If you stick with your business long enough, the day will come when your business lifestyle will be dictated more by the "business" of your business, and less by the search for new clients. In general, the more routine and boring your work days become, the more successful your business will be.

SOME THOUGHTS ON RETIREMENT

About ten years ago, I started to get serious about saving money for the future. I was forty-two years old at the time, and my financial advisors told me that I had a lot of catching up to do. They said I needed to set aside *$1,200 per month* if I wanted to retire by age sixty. During our previous conversations, I had never said that I wanted to retire by age sixty or sixty-five. They just assumed that this would be my goal because that's the norm. I told them that I had no plans to *ever* retire as long as I was healthy. I asked them to build my personal financial portfolio based on my desire to live comfortably with little income after age eighty. My financial advisors looked at me as if I was from another planet. I looked at them in much the same way.

If I had my choice, I would eliminate the word "retirement" from the dictionary, because I believe that retirement is a very destructive end goal. To work towards retirement is to work for a time when you will have absolutely nothing to do for the rest of your life. Words like "departure," "leaving," "giving up work," and "withdrawal" are the words that we associate with retirement. As my cousin Tom Casey once said, "You must have a better ambition in life than to be the healthiest person in a nursing home."

Again, it is more important for me to enjoy the quality of my journey through life than to work towards the end goal of that journey. My personal goal is to *never* retire, but instead to continue working professionally for as long as I am healthy and able to do so. Chronological age is of little interest to me. This is a **lifestyle decision** that I have made, and it dictates how I run my business.

Many people I know seem to think that retirement *is* (or should be) the end result of their journey through life. If you ask someone with an eight-to-five, five-day-a-week job about retirement, they will usually tell you, "I'd like to retire by the time I'm fifty-five or sixty-five." Very often, what they *really* mean is "I want to stop working," or "I don't want to work at my job anymore, after a certain age." Many of these people are working in a repressed job and, like prisoners, are marking the days until they get out. The sad thing is, they are in a *self-imposed prison*, without bars and with no possibility for parole.

I ask, "Why retire at all?"

Why would anyone want to retire at fifty-five anyway? At fifty-five, statistics show that you will more than likely live at least another thirty to forty years. What are you going to do with that time? Play shuffleboard? Play golf? Visit the grandchildren? Are you going to be in a reactive mode or a proactive mode? Retirement is also hard on society because it requires other people to support you, even though you are still perfectly able to contribute to the world, both mentally and physically. If you are healthy and able to keep working, retirement shouldn't be a goal at all.

> **If you are healthy and able to keep working, retirement shouldn't be a goal at all.**

Again, I am a former Executive Director of the Puget Sound Chapter of the Alzheimer's Association and have published my own newspaper directed towards older adults. The people that I have observed who age most successfully are those who are goal-oriented and remain active, either in their chosen profession or in another activity that stimulates their mind long after what is considered to be the age of retirement.

Much of the research geared towards unlocking the mysteries of aging shows that lifestyle choices are major factors for living well, both mentally and physically, and that the people who age successfully are those who stay engaged. In other words, one must have a greater incentive to get out of bed in the morning other than being first in line for the Grand Slam special at Denny's. (If you are interested in pursuing the subject of aging further, pick up a copy of *Successful Aging* by John W. Rowe and Robert L. Kahn.)

There is another group of would-be retirees that we should perhaps mention here: Those who want to become millionaires. If you ask someone who is starting their own business, and who believes that they have the next "can't-do-without-it, everyone's-gotta-have-it" software product, they will often tell you, "I want to retire by the time I'm forty." What they *really* mean is "I want to be rich" or "I want to be financially secure for the rest of my life." In other words, they would like to earn enough money to be able to quit work and retire *whenever they want to.*

It might be good for these would-be entrepreneurs to remember that the most successful business people in the world very rarely "retire." Executives who have founded their own business and built it into a multimillion-dollar corporation typically don't "chuck it all" at age forty to go play golf. They usually stick around at the company they've created and serve as CEO or on the Board of Directors for a number of years. Or if they grow tired of the business, they may turn it over to their junior executives and go start *another* business, building it up from scratch as they did with the first one.

Even the richest man in the world, Bill Gates, has no plans to retire. He still takes a lead role in the business dealings of Microsoft. And, having realized that he can't take his money with him when he dies (*"What?!* You mean they don't accept stock options in Heaven?"), he is now in the process of giving it away. Through the Bill and Melinda Gates Foundation, he is using his money to fund medical research, educational programs, scholarships, and charities.

If you start your own business, it should of course be doing something that you enjoy. Whether that is creating ad campaigns, developing new software, or selling fortune cookies on the Internet, there's no reason for you to stop doing what you enjoy when you reach fifty-five—even if you *do* make a million dollars before then. If you are open to shifting your mindset away from retirement as being your primary goal in life, this book will be of great value to you. That change in attitude can dictate how you structure your business, and in turn, your lifestyle.

CHAPTER FIVE

Experience Is the Key

You might think that because you don't have a traditional *"strong business background,"* starting your own business is beyond your grasp. This is wrong. Again, I am living proof that you don't need an M.B.A. to be a successful businessman. I graduated from Washington State University with a degree in political science. While at Washington State, I also took a number of communications and political science courses, but I don't remember ever taking any business courses. When it comes to making your business succeed, good judgment and organization skills are far more important than an M.B.A.

But good judgement and organization skills take time to acquire. I strongly believe that *experience* is a major factor for starting a successful business. Understand, I am not talking about business experience, although it certainly doesn't hurt if you have some. I am talking about *life experience*. The more you know about the way things work—on the job, at home, and in the world in general—the better equipped you will be to start your own business. Unfortunately, experience is an attribute that you can only acquire with age.

EXPERIENCE IS ACQUIRED

The Civil War movie *Glory* makes a great point about experience. The movie tells the story of the 54th Massachusetts Infantry, the first all-African-American regiment to serve in the United States Army. In one scene, the regiment recruits have just been issued their musket rifles and are taking target practice. One soldier, Private Jupiter Sharts (played by Jihmi Kennedy), is able to hit the bullseye consistently. His fellow soldiers (who include Denzel Washington, Morgan Freeman, and Andre Braugher) are impressed with his marksmanship. Private Sharts explains proudly that he learned how to shoot while hunting squirrels.

The regiment commander, Colonel Robert Gould Shaw (Matthew Broderick), who earlier in the film was wounded in the hellish battle of Antietam, notices this. He instructs Private Sharts to reload his rifle and fire it as quickly as he can. "A good soldier can load and fire his rifle three times in one minute," Shaw tells the assembled soldiers. Private Sharts quickly reloads his rifle, pouring gunpowder from his powder horn onto the flintlock, and using a ramrod to push the bullet down the long barrel. As he does this, Colonel Shaw suddenly pulls out a pistol and begins firing gunshots in the air just behind Sharts's ear, *simulating the sounds that the soldiers will hear in battle*. Sharts becomes disoriented and nervously drops his rifle.

Colonel Shaw's lesson to his troops in this scene is that they will only become effective soldiers once they have experienced the chaos and ear-splitting noise of battle firsthand. It is one thing to stand on a firing range and score a bullseye on a target fifty yards away, and under ideal conditions. It is something else to load your rifle, aim at a moving target, shoot, and then *reload* your rifle in the middle of a real battle. The point is, *experience is something that can only be acquired, not learned*.

As with soldiers in battle, a certain amount of experience is necessary to be an effective business owner (although hopefully, as a business owner, you'll never have to load and fire a musket).

You can put together a dynamic business plan with a timetable for creating your products and/or building your clientele, and rosy projections for annual increased profits over the next five years. But the real challenge is to make it work.

There are dozens of factors—everything from local and national economic growth to marketability of your product or service, from the corporate calendars of your clients to your annual decrease or increase of expenses—that will affect your business. The more you know about your own business, and about the world in general, the better prepared you will be to start your own business and sustain it for the long run.

> If I were to pick an ideal age for a person to start their own business, I would say that they should be in their early to mid-thirties.

The best time to start your own business is when you have some experience under your belt.

WHEN SHOULD YOU START YOUR OWN BUSINESS?

If I were to pick an ideal age for a person to start their own business, I would say that they should be in their early to mid-thirties.

No one should try to start a business right out of college (or worse, right out of high school). A college education will give you the facts you need, but not the experience. Understand, I'm not saying you *shouldn't* go to college. Having *any* college degree will serve you well in starting your own business. And higher education teaches you necessary skills like discipline, organization, and option thinking (a *very* necessary skill when you have your own business).

But higher education is usually more about theory than actual job experience. For example, if you have just earned a B.S. in marketing, chances are you know the *fundamentals* of marketing.

But if someone asked you to put together a marketing campaign for a new brand of toothpaste, or a line of color copiers, or for an investment firm, you would *not* be able to do it right. You might be able to manage the individual elements—e.g., market research, brand design, advertising and promotion planning—but you would lack the experience needed to create an effective marketing campaign from scratch. Only by getting a marketing-related job, and by learning on the job how to organize a marketing campaign, will you acquire the skills you need to start your own marketing consulting business.

In your twenties, you are still figuring out what you want to do in life, and also what you *don't* want to do in life. Give yourself time to experiment, to see what type of career or which area of your chosen profession is right for you. Then, once you've decided, learn how to do your job right before you try to make a business out of it.

When you reach your mid-thirties, you have typically acquired the "street smarts" that it takes to start a business and make it grow. Whatever profession you have chosen, you now have enough experience in it to call yourself an "expert" in your field. If you are an advertising agent, you have probably worked for several agencies, creating ad campaigns. If you want to start a telecom consulting service, you have probably worked for several telecommunications companies and are familiar with the current technologies. If you want to sell wooden boats, cat toys, alpaca sweaters, etc., you may already be creating and/or selling your product in your spare time and would like to go full-time with your business.

Also, in your thirties, you know how to "have a job." You know how to plan your work, organize each task, and get it done in such a way as to meet your deadlines or quotas. You know how to have an effective meeting with your supervisors, how to talk with them and listen to them, and how to satisfy them with your job performance. When they aren't satisfied, you probably know how to analyze your work and correct the problem to their satisfaction. (As a self-employed business owner, these kinds of skills will serve you well in dealing with your clients or customers.)

You may have even *lost* a job or two, at some point. Perhaps you've been fired or laid off or had an employment contract end too soon due to a budget cut or an employer's bad whim. Believe it or not, this is good! If you were able to get back on your feet and find a new job, you have experience in "coming back." That is, you know how to rebuild your life and your career after suffering a setback. (And if you've ever been fired from a job for a mistake that you made, at least you know what that mistake is and can avoid making it again in the future.)

In your thirties, you also have enough *life experience* to know how the world works. You know how to manage your personal schedule. You enjoy being around people and can talk to them easily. You have probably exercised judgement in making some major lifestyle decisions, such as what type of house or car to buy, or whether or not to go back to school for an advanced degree. If you are married and have kids, you

> **Life-experiences help you keep your perspective in bad times and in good times.**

are used to managing daily responsibilities, even under chaotic situations (which are more or less constant when you have kids).

With your life experience, you have probably developed a *perspective* on the world—that is, a way of seeing how the world works and how your life works. You can look into the future and see the possible outcomes and potential consequences of your courses of action. A good perspective of your life will serve you well as a self-employed business owner. It will enable you to see your business for what it is and how well or how badly it is doing.

As a self-employed business owner, I have lived on very little income and I have lived with plenty of income. I know what it is like to make serious choices about whether to stay in business or close the doors. I have felt the pain and made it through the rough spots. All this experience has given me some perspective on how to start a business and keep it going through hard times. Perspective is an extremely valuable attribute.

Running your business day to day is raw. You are never more exposed. Success and failure are both very evident and decisive. Either you eventually make it or you don't. It can be a very long or short struggle. But if you don't adhere to certain basic principles, your business will eventually die. Guaranteed! The bottom line is: Life experiences help you keep your perspective in bad times and in good times.

A WORD ABOUT BACKGROUND

While actual business experience isn't necessary for starting your own business, your prospects for success may be enhanced if your parents or a close friend has succeeded in starting their own business. If so, you may have been in a position to watch the trials and tribulations of being a business owner. I know many people who have grown up in a business environment who have no desire to start their own business because of what they observed—late nights, no family time, no vacations, no money, no father, no mother, etc. They tell themselves it's just not worth it. But if you grew up in a business environment, you are in a far better position to know the psychological and emotional aspects of sustaining a business. You are also in a position to know some of the pitfalls that business owners can fall into and possibly how to avoid them.

But again, if you have no business background in your family, it doesn't necessarily put you at a disadvantage. I myself do not come from a business family. My father worked for the same medium-sized company for most of his working years. My mother was a homemaker. I didn't grow up in an environment where my parents or my brothers were slugging it out every day with the challenges of running a business. My younger brother did launch his own business several years earlier than I, but we didn't discuss business very much when we were growing up.

It wasn't until I was in my early thirties that I seriously began to think about going into business for myself. At the time, I was serving as the Executive Director of the Puget Sound chapter of the Altzheimer's Association. Before that, I had worked as a marketing and communications specialist with various public relations firms and with city and state government agencies in Seattle and Olympia, Washington. The idea of starting my own business had appeared on my personal radar screen, but the thought of taking such a huge step terrified me.

What finally made up my mind for me was a book that I read, which suggested that the best time to start a business was in your early to mid-thirties. (I have long since forgotten the title or the author of this book.) Somehow that recommendation came at the exact right time, because I remember it having a profound impact on me. I decided at that very moment to quit wavering and get on with the business of starting my own business. I never looked back.

LEARNING FROM MISSTEPS AND MISTAKES

We all have regrets. As we get older, we can look back with some perspective and see how we might have done things differently. The only outcome we can hope for is that when we failed, we learned from that failure and took corrective action the next time we were confronted with similar circumstances.

I have a personal maxim that you cannot call a mistake a "mistake" unless you allow yourself to make it more than once. The first time you make a certain mistake, it is really a "misstep." You have no previous experience that you can use as a point of reference. As a business owner, you must make decisions all the time, and some of your decisions will turn out to be wrong. Your wrong decisions are the "missteps," the experiences that you learn from. Later on, when a similar situation arises in your business, hopefully you'll know better than to make the same "misstep" a second time. But if you don't learn from your previous "misstep," if you allow yourself to make the same "misstep" the second time around, then it's a "mistake!"

What do I mean by this? Well, here's an example from my own experience. As I've already mentioned, many years ago when

> **But if you don't learn from your previous "misstep," if you allow yourself to make the same "misstep" the second time around, then it's a "mistake!"**

I was publishing my newspaper, one of my advertisers, a retirement center, went out of business without paying me and stuck me with a printing bill for $10,000. Before this retirement center went bankrupt, I started noticing "trouble signs"—late payments, unreturned phone calls, etc. But I continued to extend them credit by running their ads in my newspaper. That was my "misstep." I didn't see that my client was having financial trouble until it was too late.

Then, about ten years later, I had a similar experience. I was working with a travel agency, developing radio ad campaigns and buying air time for their commercials. As part of my service to my clients, I normally purchase air time "on credit" from the radio stations that I work with. In other words, the radio stations reserve the air time and run the commercials. The client then pays me after the commercials have run, and I pay the radio stations. If ever a client *doesn't* pay me, then *I* have to pay the radio stations for the air time out of my own pocket. If I don't, it can seriously damage my relationship with those radio stations and my chances of future air time credit with them.

I started to notice some of the same "trouble signs" with the travel agency that I had noticed with my previous client who went bankrupt. The travel agency was suddenly very late in making payments to me. Their payments started arriving every two to three months, instead of once a month as usual. I sensed that the travel agency was having financial troubles. So after being paid in full for my most recent ad campaign, I informed the owner of the travel agency that I would have to receive the money for future ad campaigns up-front if I was to continue our relationship. The owner said he could not do this. I wished him well but said I could no longer work with his company. A few months later, I received a notice in the mail that the travel agency had declared bankruptcy.

By reading the "trouble signs" correctly, I avoided making the same "misstep" with the travel agency that I had made with the retirement center. If I had kept on doing business with the travel agency, even after my experience with the previous client, *THAT* **would have been a mistake!** If the travel agency had gone out of business without paying me, I would once again have been forced to pay my vendors, in this case the radio stations, out of my own pocket. But because of my previous experience with the other client, I was able to avoid making this "mistake."

PUTTING PEOPLE OUT TO PASTURE IN THEIR PRIME

One of the biggest shames in our society is that people with experience are put out to pasture in their prime. Even though the fifty-plus population controls 80 percent of the nation's assets, advertisers barely notice the aging population. We are a very youth-driven culture. There is nothing you can do about this, but if you are a member of the fifty-plus population, there are some things you can do to ensure that age discrimination doesn't affect you. Starting your own business is one of these things.

During the latter part of the twentieth century, companies made a habit of laying off people in their fifties and sixties to make way for a younger work force. Demographically, the world has changed dramatically in the last thirty years and there is an actual shortage of qualified workers. But we still can't seem to shake the mindset that older workers are past their prime and therefore have nothing valuable to contribute. Youthful energy is important, but it must be tempered with knowledge and experience.

> **If you are going into battle, not listening to a person with battle experience could cost you your life. In business, it could cost you your business.**

It may sound obvious, but I believe that anyone who is thinking about starting their own business should talk with *and listen to* someone who has already started a similar business. I have seen many people and businesses that did not value the experience of others, and it has cost them dearly. Very often, after their business has gone under, these people talk with other, more experienced people in their field and learn some valuable fact or technique that might have saved them. "Gee, if I'd known *this* or *that*, I might still be in business now!"

If you are going into battle, not listening to a person with battle experience could cost you your life. In business, it could cost you your business.

CHAPTER SIX

———⇒⊰●⊱⇐———

Lessons From the Dot-Com Crash

When I speak of learning from experience, I am not just talking about learning from your *own* mistakes. And when I talk about learning from the experiences of others, I don't mean just learning from those who have been *successful* in business. You can learn just as much, if not more, by studying the *failures.* Often, an analysis of businesses that have failed can tell you what *not* to do in your own business and can clue you in to the pitfalls and traps that entrepreneurs should avoid.

In the late 1990's, as Internet access became available to almost everyone, a new type of entrepreneurial business, the "dot-com start-up," started to emerge. If something could be sold, traded, or transacted over the Internet, an entrepreneur would find a way to do it. Investors and venture capitalists lined up in droves, pouring billions of dollars into dot-com start-ups in the hopes of cashing in on the Internet craze and the so-called "New Economy."

Unfortunately, many of the dot-coms are now jokingly (and sadly) referred to as "dot-gones." As long as the economy was good, investors were more than willing to pour money into dot-coms. The Internet was seen as "the next big thing," a better and faster way to do business, trade goods and services, and move information. But when the national economy started to cool down, many investors stopped putting their money into dot-coms that were spending millions of dollars a day and still not turning a profit. It became known as the "burst of the dot-com bubble." Since then, dozens of dot-com start-ups have gone out of business.

What are some of the reasons the dot-coms failed? Let me count the ways.

If the burst of the dot-com bubble teaches us anything, it's that even "New Economy" businesses must still obey "Old Economy" rules. Again, Rule #1 is, "A business must take in more money than it spends." When all is said and done, the Internet is nothing more than an extremely useful communications tool. An Internet-based business must *still* offer a tangible product or service and must still make an actual profit if the business is to survive.

Even if you don't plan to start an Internet-based business, you can still learn a lot about what *not* to do as a self-employed business owner by studying the mistakes of the dot-com era. What are some of the reasons the dot-coms failed? Let me count the ways:

1. They used other people's money (that is, the money given to them by investors) and lots of it. When you use other people's money to build your business, it becomes frighteningly easy to spend. You develop bad habits, such as not accounting for each dollar. Also, when someone else is financing you, you don't have that sense of urgency to make your business successful and profitable as soon as possible. There is such a thing as having too much money when you start your business (more on this later).

2. The idea behind many dot-coms was to build their business based on the novelty of Internet technology, not

on the product or service being offered. Many dot-com entrepreneurs were not interested in offering a quality product or service, but in how they could leverage that product or service into quick money or an IPO.

3.   Many dot-coms tried to "conquer the world" with their product or service before they really understood it or before they had fully tested their concept. They spent millions of advertising dollars trying to capture "market share"—that is, trying to outdo their competitors to be the top search engine, or ISP, or online toy seller on the Internet—when they hadn't yet perfected their concept or their service or figured out how to turn it into a profitable enterprise.

4.   In many cases, dot-coms invested money in unnecessary expenditures, such as high salaries, lavish office furniture, and elaborate corporate events.

5.   Many dot-com CEO's were overnight wonder kids in their twenties who lacked the *perspective* and *experience* that it takes to start a successful business. A few more people with gray hairs around the water cooler would have helped enormously.

Now I have a confession to make. I was not immune to the "gold rush mentality" of the dot-com era. In the late 1990's, I had more "disposable" income to invest with than at any other time in my life. I invested some of my money in dot-coms, but my investments were very limited because I was always very skeptical about the long-term success of many of these ventures. As a result, when these dot-coms went out of business, I lost *some* money, but not much.

The first time I heard the term "burn rate" was at a stockholder's meeting in the year 2000, from the CEO of an Internet start-up that I had invested in. I had to ask a fellow investor what the term meant. He said that it was the money that feeds the monthly cash flow to the negative, but which the company needs in order to brand its product in the marketplace, with the goal of bringing in new investors.

In other words, the company was furiously spending more money than it was making in an effort to attract investors with more money to spend. By bringing in new investors as quickly as possible, the company hoped to offset its massive business costs until it could establish itself enough to turn a profit. In doing this, the company had created a *corporate culture of losing money.*

Unfortunately, this company's investors, myself included, soon grew very tired of hearing about the "burn rate." In essence, the company was asking us to believe the concept "We're not losing money! We're just spending more than we earn as we move towards making a profit." (This is like an airline pilot telling the passengers, "Don't worry, folks! The plane is not crashing! It's just that the rate of decent is faster than we'd like!") As investors like myself stopped believing in the "burn rate" mentality, they stopped investing, and the company went out of business.

The problem with building a culture of losing other people's money on a monthly basis is that you don't stay focused on the core of the business. The dot-com crusade failed because the people in charge believed that the red-hot economy and the lust of investors for anything Internet-related would last forever. There is always a day of reckoning in any start-up venture, where the company has to *prove* that it is making a profit. If investors see that a company is losing money over an extended period of time, they will stop investing in it. Many dot-commers were caught completely off guard when their investors suddenly cut off their cash flow. By that time, most of the dot-coms were so far in debt that they had no choice but to file for bankruptcy.

In retrospect, it's easy to see that many of the dot-coms were actually *set up to fail.* Many of these companies violated almost every principle about starting a successful long-term business that is outlined in this book. The sad part is, many of these dot-com companies *could have made it* if they had kept their overhead low and had tested and perfected their concept over time. When owners and investors get greedy, or try to do too much too soon with their business, it usually leads to disaster.

A CASE STUDY: THE WEBVAN/ HOMEGROCER PHENOMENON

Webvan.com and HomeGrocer.com both started out in the late 1990's with the concept of an Internet-based home-delivery grocery service. Both companies hoped to revolutionize the American grocery industry by doing away with the traditional "brick-and-mortar" supermarket. There was no longer any need, they argued, to waste time going to the supermarket to shop for food. Online shoppers could now order groceries on the Internet and have them delivered right to their homes the very same day.

HomeGrocer was founded in Seattle in 1998 by Terry Drayton, a software entrepreneur from Toronto. Webvan was founded that same year in San Francisco by Louis Borders, founder of Borders Books. Both companies attracted a number of high-profile investors. Webvan's investors included CBS and Knight-Ridder Newspapers; HomeGrocer's investors included Amazon.com and Martha Stewart Inc. Both companies promised that they could achieve profitability within a few years by eliminating the need for an actual supermarket store and by automating the "outdated" infrastructure of the grocery industry with high-tech distribution centers.

Within a year of going online, both companies started to aggressively expand their operations. HomeGrocer began offering grocery service in Portland, Oregon, and Orange County, California; Webvan began offering its grocery service in Los Angeles and San Diego, and later in Atlanta, Chicago, and Dallas. Both companies competed heavily with each other for market share, and also competed with established super-market chains like Safeway and Albertson's.

In June, 2000, Webvan bought out and merged with HomeGrocer, in the hopes that a larger company could achieve profitability more quickly and would attract more potential investors. But the national economy was cooling, and investors had already started to pull their money out of dot-coms that were still posting massive losses. In an effort to stay in business, Webvan consolidated or shut down several of its distribution centers and laid off almost 900 employees. But this last-ditch effort failed. On July 10, 2001, with no further investors offering money to help them continue their operations, Webvan filed for bankruptcy. At the time, they were over $800 million in debt!

What happened? Again there were so many fatal flaws that a whole series of books could be written about the Webvan/HomeGrocer debacle. The potential business owner can learn a number of lessons from studying this business fiasco:

1. **Know your business. Don't go into a business that you know nothing about.**

The founders of Webvan and HomeGrocer knew *nothing* about the infrastructure of the grocery business or about the needs of its customers. Like many dot-commers, they assumed that the *technology* would be the star of their business—not the groceries or the home delivery. They used the novelty of ordering groceries over the Internet to attract investors and hoped that this same novelty would attract customers to shop at their web sites. As it turned out, this novelty wore off very quickly, for both investors and customers.

2. **Know your market—and its limits.**

As far as I know, neither Webvan nor HomeGrocer ever did any research to identify their core market. They simply assumed that, with the current Internet craze, *everyone* would abandon the hassle of supermarket shopping for the more convenient online grocery service. If they had done a bit of market research, both companies might have been surprised at people's attitudes about grocery shopping—and about the Internet in general.

In the late 1990's, people were just starting to understand the Internet itself! The World Wide Web was a fascinating medium, but it was also a bit scary. Was it *really* safe, we wondered, to order books or CDs or groceries online? Or would there be hackers waiting inside these web sites, ready to steal our ID's and credit card numbers? It was unrealistic for Webvan and HomeGrocer to rely exclusively on the Internet as a means for recruiting and establishing their customer base. They expected grocery shoppers to use a tool that they didn't quite trust yet for everyday shopping.

When it comes to shopping for groceries, most of us simply *prefer* to go to the supermarket! We want to *see, smell, and touch the food* before we buy it. We need to see for ourselves that the fruit is fresh, that the bread is not stale, that none of the dozen eggs inside the carton are broken, and that the plastic-wrapped ground beef is pink and not past its expiration date. (It's *food*, after all! We need to make sure it's okay before we put it in our mouths.) Shopping online does not give us this same experience. As *Seattle Times* columnist Nicole Brodeur put it, "You can't squeeze tomatoes when you shop online."

I think the best target market for an online grocery delivery service would be people living in major metropolitan areas who don't have time to shop for themselves. This would include young single professionals, young professional married couples, and people who are unable to get out of the house due to injury or sickness. There *is* a market for online grocery delivery. (At its height, HomeGrocer had 30,000 customers in the Seattle area.) But it is a *niche* market.

As for other potential customers, in time people will become more comfortable with online shopping. Some of them may eventually become regular customers for online grocery services. But it takes *a long time*, not to mention a huge cash outlay, to change people's attitudes and hook them onto the convenience of a new type of service. We have been shopping at grocery stores for over one hundred years. It is unrealistic to think that we will give up this habit any time soon.

3.   Don't try to reinvent the wheel.

When I first heard of HomeGrocer.com, I assumed that its founders were approaching supermarket chains like Safeway, Krogers, and Albertson's and offering to fill a niche market by providing these companies with an online grocery service for their established customer base. I thought the concept had real possibilities.

My assumptions were wrong. Instead of trying to fill a small niche market, HomeGrocer and Webvan both decided *to build their own grocery companies from scratch*. They spent millions of dollars building huge food warehouses known as "distribution centers." They bought fleets of delivery trucks and hired thousands of employees to process and deliver orders. They hired software experts to create their online web pages and to create exclusive software to run their distribution centers faster and more efficiently than regular grocery stores.

With such high overhead, it's no wonder that both companies incurred the high levels of debt that eventually forced them into bankruptcy! In addition to building their own grocery businesses, Webvan and HomeGrocer also had to build their *customer base* from scratch. Being so new to the market, they could not rely on an existing customer base to support their business. They had to go out and try to recruit new customers away from established grocery chains. As we've already seen, this turned out to be a losing battle.

Why did Webvan and HomeGrocer feel obliged to spend millions of dollars to try to create new grocery empires from scratch? Quite simply, the founders of both companies thought that they could do it better. They believed that the national network of food warehouses that supplies supermarket chains like Albertson's and Safeway was outdated. They thought that by creating high-tech distribution centers with facilities powered by state-of-the-art software, they could provide customers with faster grocery delivery service than the supermarkets.

As it turned out, the network of food warehouses that supplies brick-and-mortar grocery chains, while it may be several decades old, is still very efficient. Again, it goes back to the founders of HomeGrocer and Webvan not knowing much about the grocery business. Their high-tech distribution centers may have worked well, but their state-of-the-art infrastructure meant little when they didn't have enough of a customer base to sustain their business.

4.   **Start slow, build slow. Don't try to "conquer the world" all at once.**

As mentioned, Webvan and HomeGrocer started to expand their business into new markets while they were still competing with each other. By offering services in metropolitan areas across the country, they hoped to grab as much market share as possible. They also hoped to attract new investors by proving that online grocery companies could compete with the established brick-and-mortar grocery chains on a national level.

In the end, however, ambition was their downfall. In the year 2000, after merging with HomeGrocer, executives at Webvan decided to offer their online grocery service in Atlanta, Dallas, and Chicago. In 2001, they built huge distribution centers, each costing several million dollars, in Dallas and Atlanta—only to close them down a few months after they had opened, when the company started to run out of money.

This is evidence of the "burn rate" in action. It cost Webvan so much money to move into a new market like Atlanta or Dallas that, by the time they had established a headquarters in that area, they had no money left to start the business. In the end, Webvan cared more about acquiring market share from its competitors than about offsetting its overwhelming profit-loss ratio.

A better scenario for establishing an online grocery service would have been to prove that it could work and survive in *one* city before moving it into other markets. Again, it would be easier to do this by offering an online service from a well-established supermarket chain with an existing customer base. Perhaps in the first year, 2 percent of the supermarket chain's customers would use the online option to order groceries on the Internet. The following year, it might be 3 percent. Perhaps in five years, 15 percent of the chain's customer base would be using the online option. In the meantime, the supermarket chain would continue to function as it always has, with customers shopping at local stores in the traditional way.

5.   **Test your concept and perfect it as much as possible before you offer it.**

Webvan and HomeGrocer encountered numerous software problems in putting their grocery services online. Many customers became impatient with slow Internet service and discovered that it was, in fact, faster to go to the supermarket and buy groceries, rather than to sit at their computer for hours and place an order online. Some customers also found that, due to web site compatibility issues, they couldn't access Webvan's pages using major web browsers like America Online.

Webvan and HomeGrocer also had problems with their delivery services. One problem unique to grocery deliveries is that someone has to be *at home* to receive the order when it is delivered. Unlike packages that contain books or software, groceries can't be left in a mailbox or deposited on a doorstep where a dog or a squirrel might get them. At the time of their closing, Webvan still had not figured out a solution to this problem.

Also, Webvan and HomeGrocer both had delivery problems in their chosen start-up cities. San Francisco and Seattle are both built on very narrow peninsulas that are crowded with hills and surrounded by large bodies of water. This makes the lay-out of streets somewhat haphazard, and traffic problems in both cities are especially bad. In both cases, delivery drivers had trouble making their same-day deliveries on time—especially when all delivery orders were filled out of one single distribu-tion center located on the outskirts of the city.

Incidentally, since the closing of Webvan/HomeGrocer, Safeway and Albertson's have had better luck with their web-based home delivery service. All orders that are made online are delivered to the customer from supermarkets located within that customer's immediate neighborhood. The delivery driver is usually a local resident who knows the streets and can navigate them easily, and thus find the customer's delivery address with-out any trouble.

6.   If you have a good brand name, <u>keep it!</u>

When Webvan.com took over HomeGrocer.com in 2000, one of the first things they did was to get rid of the HomeGrocer name and peach logo. It might have been better for the company if they had kept "HomeGrocer" and done away with the "Webvan" name and logo instead.

By the time it was bought out by Webvan, HomeGrocer had established brand recognition in its hometown. People in and around Seattle were used to seeing HomeGrocer's peach-colored delivery trucks with the company's peach-shaped logo on the side. The peach logo gave everyone who saw it an instantly recognizable symbol of the company and what it offered. When Webvan bought out HomeGrocer, it replaced the peach-logo delivery trucks with its own trucks featuring Webvan's logo, a giant blue-and-green "WV." This logo, of course, told the people who saw it nothing about the com-pany or what they offered.

But even worse than dropping HomeGrocer's logo, Webvan chose to drop the HomeGrocer *name!* As with the peach logo, the name "HomeGrocer" gives the potential customer an instant idea of what kind of products and services the company offers. On the other hand, the name "Webvan" gives no indication that the company is an Internet-based grocery delivery service. Someone who had never heard of Webvan might think it was an Internet-based furniture moving service or an overnight shipping service—or perhaps even an online traveling spider show!

7. **Never confuse the *concept* of your business with the *reality*.**

The founders of Webvan and HomeGrocer had a viable business concept with their online grocery service. The problem was, they were *too much in love with the concept itself*. They did not see the company as a business, but rather as a slick, high-tech innovation to be sold to investors. The Webvan and HomeGrocer founders believed that all they had to do to stay in businesses was to keep selling their concept to investors until their companies eventually turned a profit. But when the investors stopped buying the concept, both companies started to fall apart.

It takes much more than a great idea to start a business and keep it going for the long run. A business must be treated as a business if it is to survive. Innovative technology and new ways to sell products can't take the place of common sense and good judgement. The Webvan and HomeGrocer founders created a business where selling a concept took precedence over perfecting that concept, and where establishing market share over well-established competitors became more important than turning a profit. In the end, this combination of little experience, excessive overhead, too much money, and little accountability proved to be a disaster for both companies.

CHAPTER SEVEN

Judgment

Nothing has disappeared from the American landscape during my lifetime faster than good judgment. You can read all the books, including this one, about starting your own business, but in the end your success or failure comes down to whether you exercise good or bad judgment. If you exercise good judgment more often than bad, you have a good chance of succeeding. Unfortunately, like experience, good judgment can't be taught. By the time you are in your twenties or thirties, you have either acquired good judgment or you haven't.

Have you exercised good judgment when you've been in charge of your life? Do you demonstrate good judgment in choosing your friends and associates? How about in the jobs you've taken, or in the lifestyle choices you've made? How many times have your business or personal relationships ended in mistrust, or in contempt for the other person or organization? We all have some baggage, but do you have a history of making bad judgment calls or repeating the same mistakes?

On the other hand, if you feel that, by and large, you've been happy with your choices in life, and if you are a person who has generally exercised good judgment, there is a very good chance that you will succeed in business.

"GENIUS IS GUESSING RIGHT"

Lou Tice, the co-founder of the Pacific Institute, along with his wife Diane, once said, "Genius is guessing right." The skill of guessing right can be as impactful as correctly speculating that the moon's surface would support a manned spacecraft. How did anyone know for sure that the surface of the moon was durable enough to withstand the thrust and weight of the Apollo spacecraft? There was a tremendous amount of research to support this belief, but until July 20, 1969, when the Eagle lunar module touched down at Tranquility Base, it was still all conjecture. The researchers who studied the moon's surface guessed right, and there are two astronauts who are very glad they did.

Guessing right can just be a matter of studying all the facts and possibilities that you have on hand and making a decision based on the most logical course of action. But guessing right also involves a certain amount of risk-taking. You must trust your own judgement enough to say, "Now is the time to expand my business into this market." Or "I don't think I should work with this company, even though they have been very successful. There's something about their business practices that I don't quite trust." Or "I'd better make this deal now, because in a year or so, I think it will turn out to be very profitable." Again, whether you are running a restaurant or a software company, the more you guess right, the more you will succeed.

BUSINESS IS ABOUT MAKING MONEY

One of the most important factors in building a successful business is to exercise good judgment when it comes to managing your money.

John F. Kennedy once said, "Victory has many friends; losers are like orphans." It's like that in business. When you have the money to pay your bills, everyone is your friend. Fall behind in your payments, and suddenly it's a very lonely world. Remember that every relationship you establish in business is first and always a *business* relationship. Do not develop any illusions to the contrary.

Business is about survival. A business relationship will continue as long as you are benefiting from someone, or as long as they are benefiting financially from you. As soon as that financial incentive ends, so will the relationship. It is far more important for a client to trust and respect you than to like you. But if people trust and respect you, chances are they will probably like you as well.

You must remember that executives and businesspeople have their own agendas based primarily on making money. It is often hard for them to see you as a person, or as someone who exists outside of their business agendas. I once spent over $400,000 in advertising in one radio market in a six-week period, and I have yet to receive a thank-you note from any of the radio groups that I did business with. Collectively, the only thing that these radio groups seem to focus on is the next media buy from my company. The only question I ever receive from their account executives is "When are you coming back into our market?" I don't think this is good business on their part, but I try to look at the situation from their perspective. I know that radio salespeople are under huge pressures to meet sales quotas, and if they fall short, they are out the door.

At times, business people seem to wear blinders. They see the glass as half-empty when it is really half-full—or even three-quarters full! I once had a budget of about $135,000 to spend on a radio campaign in a major metropolitan region. One radio group in this particular market received over $100,000 of the buy. The rest of the radio groups in the market received a combined total of $35,000. Obviously, the radio group that received $100,000 was the largest radio group and had the most listeners that I was trying to reach on behalf of my client.

After the $100,000 radio group learned of my intended buy, I received a call from their sales manger. I thought he would be ecstatic with my decision. Instead, the first words out of his mouth were literally "This is unacceptable!" I thought for a moment that he was kidding. When I realized he was *not* joking, I said that I was expecting an important call and would have to get back to him tomorrow. I said this because I had to cool down before speaking to him. I was so angry that I was afraid I might say something I would later regret. (I have a twenty-four hour rule. If I am going to say anything negative, I will wait at least twenty-four hours.)

When I finally got back to the sales manager, he said that he felt that his radio group deserved a larger percentage of the buy in this particular market. He went on to say that the $100,000 buy would make them short of their income projections. I took notes, politely said goodbye, and hung up. Then I called a salesperson that I knew at the station and asked her to tell the sales director that if they didn't reserve the time for the radio purchase by noon that day, the whole deal was off. They reserved the time.

As I've said before, one of my major reasons for starting my own business is to achieve freedom of association, the freedom to choose the people that I will and will not work with. There are certain people with whom I just won't do business anymore. This includes people who only return your phone calls after you've called them four or five times and left messages. It also includes people who haggle over the cost of every small detail of your work for them, who keep you waiting for months on end while they make up their minds whether or not they're going to *do* the project they've hired you for, who cancel meetings with you at the last minute, and who don't send you all the material you need to do the job right. Once you've completed the job, it takes them several months to pay you. You have to keep calling them back and maybe send two or three invoices, before they send you the check that they promised to send you three weeks ago.

On the other hand, it's a real joy to work with people who pay their bills on time, so you don't wake up at 3 AM., wondering if you will get paid in time to pay your own bills. It's a pleasure to work with people who are accountable, who meet their dead-lines, always keep their word, and who go out of their way to let you know that they appreciate your business. Life is so much easier when you work with people like this. Your distress level goes down, and the quality of your journey is greatly enhanced. It is much more pleasant to do business with someone if you really like them.

READING A ROOM

One of the most valuable judgement skills that you can develop as a business owner is the ability to *read a room*. This is a form of perception that allows you to look at a person, or a group of people, and to gauge what they are thinking by their facial expressions, body language, manner of speech, and tone of voice. If you wish to succeed in business, this is an *absolutely essential skill.*

The ability to read a room will serve you well no matter what type of business you are in. If you are in sales, you will need this ability when you give a sales pitch, to determine if your audience is interested in what you have to sell. If you are in advertising, you will need to be able to read a room when you give presentations to your clients on the ad campaigns that you develop for them. You must be able to pick up on their thoughts and feelings and to sense whether they understand your ad concepts and like them. If you own a restaurant, you must be able to sense when your customers are unhappy with their food or service, even if they haven't actually made any complaints.

It's easy to spot the people who *don't* have the ability to read a room. They have all the bad habits that tick off the rest of us, while they themselves remain oblivious to the fact that they are annoying everyone else. They call you on the phone and then put you on hold. They bring their cell phones to lunch and have loud conversations during the meal. They are the people who, at a business meeting or a funeral, always just happen to say the wrong thing. And they are always the last ones to leave a party.

Being sensitive to your surroundings will help you more than any business plan in achieving success in business. Ask a spouse, friend, or acquaintance: "Am I a sensitive person? Do I know how you are feeling most of the time? When I'm in a group of people, do I say things that are out of place?" If you hear too many "Yes" answers to the last question, be very wary of going into business on your own.

> **Being sensitive to your surroundings will help you more than any business plan in achieving success in business.**

A PRESIDENT'S STORY

The best person I've ever known for reading a room is Dr. Glenn Terrell, former president of Washington State University. Dr. Terrell has an almost instinctive ability to measure the emotions and thoughts of a room full of people, no matter what the situation.

When Dr. Terrell retired as president of Washington State University in 1985, I attended his retirement dinner in Seattle. You could tell that all the people in the room had tremendous respect for this man. Everyone had an incredible story to tell about their experiences with Dr. Terrell, and the keynote speakers at the dinner praised him extensively for his leadership qualities and for his contributions to the university during his eighteen years as president.

It was getting late into the evening, and the speeches and tributes were going on far too long. People in the audience were starting to nod off, and I saw a number of heads snap back at the dinner tables surrounding me as people caught themselves falling asleep. We were all waiting for Dr. Terrell to make his remarks and thank the university for honoring him so that we could finish the evening and go home.

Finally, during one particularly long anecdote, Dr. Terrell stood up, walked across the stage, and gently took the microphone away from the speaker. We all sat up and listened. Now, at last, we were going to hear words of great wisdom from the retiring president. What was he going to say?

In his southern drawl, Dr. Terrell announced to the audience, "I don't know about you, but I am going to the restroom!"

With that he put the microphone back on the podium and walked out of the room. Almost at once, half the 400 or so people in the room—who had apparently been waiting for the same opportunity—stood up and followed him to the restrooms. Afterwards, Dr. Terrell returned to the ballroom, made a few brief remarks of thanks, and said goodnight. Talk about knowing the right thing to say at the right time!

I have seen Dr. Terrell use his ability to read a room in meetings with the Washington State University Board of Regents, with state legislative committees, and with student and alumni groups at the university. He has the ability to sense what almost everyone in the room is thinking and instinctively knows when to stop talking and listen to what someone else has to say. If a few people are dominating the discussion, he has the ability to draw out the quiet people and give them a chance to speak.

I asked Dr. Terrell to provide some insight on his ability to read a room in a recent phone interview:

Q: How do you read a room? When you walk into a room, whether it's a board meeting with ten people or a banquet hall with two hundred people, what do you look for?

Dr. Terrell: *"I look at gestures, facial expressions, body language. I listen to the words that people are saying, because what they say and* *how they say it generally conveys what they are feeling at the time. I'm an observer of human behavior."*

Q: How did you learn how to read a room? Where and when did you acquire this ability?

Dr. Terrell: *"I have a Ph.D. in psychology. I learned the general principles of behavioral science, and I've been able to apply those principles to meetings with individuals and groups. I have an interest in serving people in an effective way. You can't do that if you can't read them, if you can't understand what they are saying and what lies behind what they are saying. Effective perception leads to effective leadership.*

"My career has given me the opportunity to meet with many people and numerous organizations, which, of course, are made up of people. I was chairman of the department of psychology at University of Colorado, then dean of the College of Arts and Sciences at University of Illinois in Chicago, before serving as president of Washington State University for eighteen years. You don't last very long in those kinds of administrative positions unless you can read people very well and can work well with them."

Q: Is this something that other people can learn? Or does it require a background in psychology?

Dr. Terrell: *"No, my psychology background is only part of it. I believe that anyone can learn how to read a room by applying the techniques I've mentioned. When you walk into a room full of people, look around at what they are doing and listen to what they say. Watch their gestures, expressions, their body language. Listen for the language cues in their speech. With practice, you'll be able to read the mood of any room you walk into.*

"Some people acquire skills like this without the formal training. Some people learn how to read a room, or how to read people, at an early age through their interactions with others. My mother and father were very good at it. I've also had colleagues in my various positions who were good at reading people, and I learned from them.

"My contention of leadership is that leaders are, in fact, ministers. I wrote a book called **The Ministry of Leadership**.* *I believe that university presidents are ministers who attend to the educational and personal needs of faculty and students. To address these needs, you must be able to understand people, what their problems are, what their dreams are, what their goals in life are. So, ultimately, my ability to read a room is a combination of formal education, practical experience, and leadership theory."*

TIMING IS EVERYTHING

One of the biggest judgment calls you will make is when to launch your business. You must weigh all the factors, and decide on the best time to go into business for yourself. The factors you will need to consider might include the timeliness of your business, whether there is a demand for the product or service you offer, how much money you have to finance your entrepreneurship (and to support yourself while you build your business), and whether or not your family circumstances are open to you starting a business at that time.

Going into business is like getting married; it requires a huge commitment. Like marriage, you may want to pursue it in the future, but the timing right now may be off. It could be that now is just not the right time to be starting your business. The more you have thought through the timing of your product or service and whether you have the necessary support, the better off you will be. But there will never be the "perfect" time to start a business. There is a point where you just have to take the plunge.

ETHICS AND INTEGRITY

My parents taught me ethics and integrity, just as their parents taught them the importance of honesty. I consider myself lucky to have grown up in a family environment where doing the right thing was considered to be the *only* option. If you are a person who has to think long and hard about the difference

*Information contained in suggested reading at the back of the book.

between right and wrong, then starting a business may not be the best thing for you.

Ethics is defined as: *The rules and standards governing the conduct of members of a profession.* **Integrity** is defined as: *Strict personal honesty and independence.*

The only part of life that you have absolute control over is your word. If you work for a large organization, you can sometimes hide from ethics. Under the company umbrella, you are not considered to be entirely "at fault" for the company's unethical decisions. You may have been one of several hundred unethical decision-makers. Even if you knew that the decisions you were making were wrong, you may have been in a position where you were forced to make those decisions or lose your job.

But when you are a self-employed business owner, you are 100 percent accountable for your own actions! The only finger you can point is at yourself!

There is a point in your life where you must decide if you are going to be up-front and honest with people, or if you will do anything to make a buck. Having a creed of ethics and integrity is a conscious mindset. Your goal should be to place ethics and integrity into your *unconscious* mindset, so that this creed becomes automatic.

I have made my share of mistakes in business, but I have always made a point of adhering to ethics and integrity. If a client overpays me by even just a dollar, my accountant is under strict instructions to return the money. If I give you my word, nothing will stop me from trying to fulfill that commitment. If I fail, I will apologize and take full responsibility for my shortcomings.

ULTIMATE RATIONALISM

As I've already mentioned, many years ago when I was just starting my business, I completed a very large print job for a retirement center. After the job was distributed, the owner informed me that the retirement center was almost bankrupt, and he didn't have the money to pay me. I was obviously very angry when I heard this.

To my amazement, the owner then went on to tell me that he really hadn't done anything wrong by not disclosing the company's financial condition to me. He said, "I didn't lie to you. I just didn't disclose everything." *He had to rationalize his bad behavior.* What is absolutely frightening is that this person actually *believed* what he was saying. I have since learned that this person left so many people high and dry that he actually had to move to another city for personal safety reasons.

I do not understand the mentality of thieves and liars. In addition to being just plain wrong, it's also a very expensive way to live. Thieves and liars spend all their time running from people whom they've cheated, or dreaming up complicated schemes to cheat more people, when it would be much easier for them to get a job and earn money *honestly.* It just takes too much effort to be dishonest.

The most dangerous people in this world are those who "rationalize" their bad behavior. If you are in business for any length of time, it's not a question of *if,* but *when you will encounter these people.* Unfortunately, they are very hard to spot when you first meet them. On the surface, they appear competent and approachable, but many times you find out too late that they are irresponsible and untrustworthy.

I also hear that many people who steal and cheat are not in it for the money but do it for the thrill of the cat-and-mouse game. They obviously don't care about the real-life traumas that they cause. Computer hackers are notorious for this type of behavior.

I recently read a news article about an engineer who spent nearly a decade perfecting a software package for large engineering firms. After spending thousands of dollars to develop this package, he offered it for sale on the Internet. It was an effective piece of software, so many engineering firms were willing to pay for it, despite its high price. But just as the engineer was about to launch his business, a hacker broke into his web site, stole the software package, and offered it free of charge on another web site. When the hacker was caught, he said he hadn't been interested in making money from the stolen software. He just enjoyed the rush of stealing it over the Internet.

Why don't these people just take up rock climbing or whitewater rafting for their kicks and leave the rest of us alone?

THE "AMWAY DECEIT"

I have a standard term for any prospective business deal that does not seem quite ethical. I call it an "Amway Deceit." Basically, an "Amway Deceit" is any proposed business opportunity that promises you can make a lot of money in a short amount of time, usually by following these ten easy steps, buying these books and motivational tapes, etc. Of course, the only people who ever make any money off these schemes are the people who sell them.

About twenty years ago, I was asked to attend a party by someone I didn't know particularly well. I was a little surprised that this person was calling me out of the blue to invite me to a gathering at his house. But I am always up for a party, so I said, "Sure!"

When I got to the party, I found about a dozen people gathered there, milling around with drinks in their hands. I was introduced around the room and was just starting to settle into the flow of the evening when our host came to the center of the room and requested our attention. He asked us to take a seat, because he wanted to talk to us about something very exciting.

Strange, I thought, taking my seat, *but okay.* Then someone whom I hadn't seen at the party before, emerged from the kitchen with a flip chart in hand. He was dressed in a spiffy suit and stood out from the rest of us, who were all dressed very casually. The newcomer to the party set up his flip chart, and without introducing himself, went around the room asking each of us what we would do if we had $20,000—*right now?!* Would we buy a brand new car? How about making a down payment on a new house? How about going on that dream vacation? Perhaps we would use the money to pay off some bills!

I can't remember the rest of the presentation because at this point I was not very happy that I had been deceived. I was so angry with the host of the party that I have not spoken to him since that night.

Over time, I learned how to spot an "Amway Deceit." A person I didn't know very well would call me up with a sudden urge to take me to lunch. Or they would invite me to attend a function at their house. Whenever I got one of these calls, I immediately asked why they were suddenly being so sociable with me.

"Is this an 'Amway Deceit'?" I would ask.

"Absolutely not!" they'd assure me. "This is not an Amway meeting but an opportunity for you to own your own business!"

If I consented to meet them and let them give me their sales pitch, I would get an uneasy feeling halfway through their presentation. "This talks like Amway. It sure smells like Amway. Are you sure this isn't Amway?"

"Well, yes…it *is* Amway," they would finally admit. "But you can *still* be an independent businessperson!"

One of the last "Amway Deceit" calls I ever received came from someone that I had vaguely known in high school. I remembered him well enough to recall that we didn't have anything in common back then. The conversation went something like this:

"Hi, Paul Casey. This is Jack! Remember me from high school?"

"Hi, Jack. Does this have anything to do with Amway?"

There was a long pause on the other end of the line. Jack was so stunned that he couldn't think of what to say.

"Thanks for the call, Jack, but I'm not interested," I said. "See you at the next class reunion." And I hung up!

If you've had similar kinds of phone calls come your way, I don't have to tell you that an "Amway Deceit" is no way to run a business. *Never* use gimmicks or tricks to sell your products or services or to get your foot in the door. It will only hurt your company in the short term *and* in the long run. Your goal should be to build a class outfit based on a principle of honesty and integrity with your clients or customers, no matter how lean your business gets. An "Amway Deceit" is a great example of a sales tactic that you should avoid at all costs.

AVOIDING DISASTERS

Setbacks and missteps are an everyday part of running your own business. Usually, setbacks and missteps by themselves are not fatal. But if you aren't careful, they can multiply into disasters from which you have no chance of recovery.

Most disasters are made up of small, incremental mistakes and missteps. When we read about a human tragedy or catastrophe, we usually read about the end result of a small series of miscalculations. The 1912 sinking of the Titanic is a good example of this. In the case of the Titanic, there were plenty of miscalculations and warning signs that things were not going well. *The real tragedy is that if only one of these miscalculations or warning signs had been caught, the whole disaster might have been avoided.*

a.   The Titanic was traveling too fast through the sea on a dark, moonless night.

b.   The Titanic's crew ignored a radio warning that there were icebergs in the vicinity.

c.   The lookouts in the crow's nest, who were watching for icebergs, didn't have binoculars, which might have enabled them to spot the "fatal iceberg" in time for the ship to avoid it.

d.   Once trouble was spotted, the Titanic tried to veer away from the iceberg instead of hitting it head on. Veering away from the iceberg resulted in a huge tear in the side of the ship, causing the vessel to sink quickly.

e.   There were not enough lifeboats for the number of passengers on board.

f.   A ship in the vicinity of the sinking ocean liner ignored the Titanic's emergency flares and did not come to the rescue.

In business, there are often a number of red flags or warnings that there may be trouble ahead, but often we ignore them until it is too late to do anything about it. As an entrepreneur, you must learn to read the warning signs and to recognize when things are not going well and need correcting. You cannot simply hope that things will "get better" if you leave them alone.

For example, say your business is starting to lose its existing clients. The ones that you manage to keep are stretching out their payments, so that your cash flow is becoming tighter. Your phone calls are not being returned, and when you check your income for the last quarter, you discover that you were way off in your projections. How did this happen? Again, you can blame other people and factors beyond your control. Or you can look inside yourself, examine your actions, and see where you've gone off track.

It may be that you were losing clients because you were missing deadlines, or because your work has been sloppy, or because you weren't as accessible to your clients as you have been in the past. Maybe the product or service you are offering isn't hitting the right niche and you need to adjust your marketing plan. Whatever the reason, the fact that you *recognized* the warning signs means that you've avoided disaster. Identify the behavior that made things go astray, correct it, and move on.

One more word of warning: There are some fatal mistakes that can hurt your business beyond any series of small mistakes. These fatal errors include abdicating accountability, arrogance toward your clients, and lying. All I can say is, avoid making these fatal mistakes at all costs. They are the "icebergs" that can sink your business faster than the Titanic.

DON'T LIE...ESPECIALLY TO YOURSELF

An essential judgment call that you must continually make in building your business is to not lie, especially to yourself. When I was publishing my monthly newspaper, I was in charge of both the editorial content and the selling of advertising space. It was quite a challenge. As soon as one issue was printed, I was working on the next issue. In the newspaper business, selling advertising is the key to survival.

Early on, I had some success in attracting advertisers to the paper and I was making a living at it. It wasn't a *great* living, but I was paying my bills and had some money left over. Each month, I would make out a target list of potential clients that I thought were likely to advertise in my paper. I found myself dividing possible advertisers into two lists—one of "hot prospects" and one of "likely prospects." I interpreted the hot prospects as being in the bag. There was no reason, I thought, why they *shouldn't* want to advertise with my paper. As it turned out, the "hot prospects" list was more of a wish list than a reality list.

After adding up the hot and likely prospects at first blush, my advertising projections always looked very strong. I felt very good about where I was in relation to my projected income. Things were going well, I told myself.

Then I asked myself: "Where am I *really* at? How many potential advertisers on my list are *really* hot prospects, and how many have I actually *sold?*" When I went through the exercise again, adding up the revenue only for those clients whom I had actually sold for the next issue, the picture was very different. My potential revenues were substantially less than what I had originally projected. Often, I would have to cut the number of pages in the next issue to save on print costs and production expenses.

This was and is a very important lesson: Set your goals, *but be realistic!* If, as Lou Tice says, "genius is guessing right," then a good part of guessing right is *not guessing wrong.* Very often, when someone guesses wrong, it is because they assumed that something in their equation was a "given," when it was not. There are hundreds of ways to deceive yourself in business. It is much better to set your goals based on what you know you have now, rather than on what you *think* you will have in the future. When you lie to yourself, the consequences can be fatal.

MOST MISTAKES ARE SELF-INDUCED

Avoid as many icebergs as possible along your journey. Some icebergs exist just because of the inherent risks of being in business. It's like driving your car. Every time you are in traffic, you risk having an accident. But most collisions are accidents waiting to happen. Either you or the other party was driving too fast, following too close, or not taking bad weather or poor road conditions into account as you were driving.

It's the same with business. Most mistakes, or missteps, are self-induced. When things go wrong, it may be because you have been doing too many things at once, or because you have not been paying attention to the essentials of your business. Maybe you've been doing a little too much cruise control and not enough braking in developing your business.

Most of the missteps I've made occurred when I ventured into areas that I shouldn't have. What makes self-induced mistakes or missteps even more painful is that, in most cases, my gut instinct told me not to go in that particular direction.

For example, a few years ago, I was contacted by a non-profit organization that wanted my help in developing radio commercials for a major ad campaign. In my first conversation with the director of this non-profit, I learned that other advertising mediums besides radio would be used in the campaign. The non-profit director mentioned that he had recently appeared on a well-known national talk show, and that he wanted to use the talk show host's name and likeness in a billboard ad campaign ("As seen on TV...").

There was only one problem. The non-profit director mentioned that he hadn't contacted the talk show host for permission to use her name and likeness. He indicated that he really didn't think it was necessary to contact the talk show host before putting her picture on a billboard to endorse his organization. "As long as she doesn't object," he told me, "there's no problem."

That statement set off a warning bell in my mind. My gut instinct told me that there was something not quite right with the director's sense of business ethics. Perhaps, I thought, it would be better to turn him down. But instead of listening to my gut instinct, I decided to take the non-profit on as a client. I worked with them and developed a successful radio ad campaign for the organization.

My troubles started when I sent the non-profit an invoice for the ad campaign. The non-profit director sent me a check for $50,000, but indicated that this money was intended for the *next* radio ad campaign that I would develop for them. But they hadn't yet paid me for their *first* radio ad campaign! I cashed the $50,000 check and used it to pay the radio stations that had run the commercials for the non-profit's first campaign.

The non-profit director was furious! He filed a lawsuit against me, claiming a breach of contract and misappropriation of funds. As of this writing, I haven't heard anything about the lawsuit in two years, so I assume that it has been dropped. I have since heard that this non-profit director is currently being investigated for fraud and mismanagement of contributions to his organization, so he has a lot more to worry about than suing me. But still, it cost me $10,000 in legal fees, not to mention a whole lot of aggravation, to defend myself against the lawsuit.

If I had trusted my gut instinct, I would have turned this client down and saved myself a lot of trouble. Always trust and act on your gut instincts. If you sense that something is not right about the way that someone else conducts their business, avoid doing business with that person or company. If your gut instinct tells you that *you* are the one who is making the mistake, analyze your business or your job performance and see where the mistake lies. Once you identify the mistake, you can take action to correct it.

CRITICAL SELF-ANALYSIS

When you hit trouble spots in your life, do you usually blame other people or circumstances beyond your control? Or do you take a long look in the mirror and ask yourself, "What am *I* doing wrong here? What could *I* do differently that might produce a better result?" Business people who practice Critical Self-Analysis have a much better chance of succeeding than those who always see themselves as "the victim."

Critical Self-Analysis is the ability to look inside *yourself*, to find *your* mistakes, and to hold *yourself* accountable for them. It is not always easy to do this, but the ability to recognize your own faults and failures will serve you well in the long run. Critical Self-Analysis can be a life-saver when it comes to keeping your business going in the face of setbacks. Those who do not have this quality will eventually encounter a fatal mistake from which their business cannot recover.

IT COULDN'T BE MY FAULT... *COULD IT?*

One of the reasons that most of us are not critical self-thinkers is that we are not taught to be, or we haven't taught ourselves to be. We live in a culture that increasingly blames external forces, rather than our own shortcomings, for our lot in life. Did you fail the big exam last week in your high school class? Blame it on the teacher's teaching methods, or on the fact that the exam was held too early in the morning, or on the fact that you "just don't test well." Don't blame it on the fact that *you* were out partying with friends on the night before the exam and didn't study for it. Did you wreck your car on an old, winding road a few nights ago? Blame it on the rain that was coming down and the poor road conditions, not on the fact that *you* were doing 60 M.P.H. in a 40 M.P.H. zone.

I know a number of failed business owners who still have no clue as to why their businesses failed. Lacking the capacity for Critical Self-Analysis, they blame everyone but themselves for their failure. They never look inside themselves and ask, "What could *I* have done differently?"

Here are some examples:

> **Failed publisher**: "There just wasn't a market for my publication."
> **Observation:** "Not true. You were unable (or unwilling) to sell your publication to the *right* market."

> **Failed publisher**: "This town isn't ready for my type of publication."
> **Observation:** "That may be true—but did you notice all those typos and mistakes in your last issue? With so many typos, you are *screaming* to your audience that you don't take pride in producing your publication.

If *you* don't care about it, why should they? What about your advertisers? Do you think they want to be associated with a publication that is riddled with so many mistakes?

Failed publisher: "I was late in getting the publication printed because I missed the press time."

Observation: "As usual, you were very disorganized and were scrambling to get things done at the last moment. Your newspaper is late because it wasn't ready for printing and you missed your press time."

Critical Self-Analysis requires, first, that you acknowledge the fact that you are *capable* of making mistakes. Like everyone else, you are only human. When things go wrong, it is *probable* that you yourself have committed some error somewhere. Once you realize this, you can examine your own actions and the quality of your product or service, and hopefully *find* that error. Once you've found it, you can either take steps to correct it, or learn from your experience and avoid making the same error the next time around.

YOU and ONLY YOU are responsible for your own successes or failures.

Critical Self-Analysis requires being honest with yourself. If you are having trouble finding clients or customers, it does no good to say, "They just don't see the value of my product or service." It is better to ask yourself, "*Why* don't they see the value of my product or service? Is there something wrong with the way I'm marketing it? How can I improve my marketing message so that more people see the value of what I'm offering?" You might even ask, "Am I marketing to the wrong target audience here? Is there another group of people that might benefit more from my product or service?"

When all is said and done, YOU and ONLY YOU are responsible for your own successes or failures.

"EVERYTHING'S YOUR RESPONSIBILITY"

In the movie, *A Bug's Life*, a grasshopper tells the new Ant Queen, "The first rule of management is: Everything's your fault!"

I wouldn't go *that* far. Certainly, there will be times when you encounter mistakes or setbacks in your business that are *not* your fault, or not entirely your fault. But even if the problem did not originate with you, as a self-employed business owner, *it is still your responsibility to correct it.*

I would revise the grasshopper's statement to read, "As a business owner, everything's your *responsibility*." That is, as someone who has offered a product or service to the client, it is YOUR responsibility to correct mistakes, to overcome setbacks, and to see that your current project or business is put back on track before things get worse. No one else can do it for you.

> **It is YOUR responsibility to correct mistakes, to overcome setbacks, and to see that your current project or business is put back on track before things get worse. No one else can do it for you.**

That said, even if a mistake or setback is not entirely your fault, there is usually something that *you* can do to help correct it. For instance, say you are working with a local free agent who specializes in marketing to create an ad campaign that involves both radio commercials and direct mail pieces. The radio commercials are being written and produced on time, but the direct mail pieces are not. Perhaps you have assigned too much work to your agent, and it might be time to bring another agent in on the job to handle the overload.

Once you've identified the source of a problem, it is often easy to see the solution. But again, a bit of Critical Self-Analysis may be necessary for you to *accept* that solution. Sometimes, in order to solve a problem, you must put your ego aside and accept a solution that you might not consider otherwise. For example, you may need to step aside and let someone who has more expertise in a certain area take over part of a project, even though you consider that project to be "your baby." Being open to new possibilities and regularly dropping your ego down a few notches can go a long way towards helping to correct mistakes and overcome setbacks.

It does not matter if you are a photographer, a software developer, an architect, an astronaut, or an innkeeper. When things aren't going well, you must be able to look inside yourself and say, "What am I doing wrong here? How can I correct my own mistakes and get things back on track?" The more detached and objective you are, the better your self-assessment will be.

ACCOUNTABILITY

You either are accountable or you are not. If you don't understand accountability—or if you choose to work with too many people who are not accountable in their business dealings— your own business will eventually fail.

To me, accountability is an irrevocable part of the business mindset. It is a creed that I live by. If I give my word that I will pay a bill, I will pay it. If a vendor doesn't pay me, I will still meet my obligations to my clients. Accountability means telling my client exactly what I think, even if it means turning down a potential client because I believe that their money could be better spent elsewhere. It also means returning money to a client if what I recommended didn't bring results.

Accountability is having absolutely no ambivalence about taking sole responsibility for every aspect of your company. Accountability is standing by your product or service 100 percent. If the client is not satisfied, your only option is to offer a full refund, period.

If you hire a free agent to execute a task on your behalf, and the client is not satisfied with the agent's performance, then as the owner of the business that often times bears your name, *you* are totally responsible. After all, you hired the agent. If the unsatisfied client calls you about the free agent, you must take complete responsibility immediately and without hesitation.

Accountability also means making every effort to meet your deadlines with a client. At the beginning of a project, give your client a realistic deadline by which you will complete your work—and stick to that deadline! If you think you may miss a deadline, contact your client ahead of time and let them know that you will be late. *Never leave a client wondering when they will receive your product or service.*

If you do miss a deadline, *never* tell the client it was because you were busy with another client, or because your child was sick. *Be perfectly honest with your client about how and where you failed.* Tell your client that you underestimated the scope of the task, or that the information you needed came in slower than expected. Show your clients that you are aware of and accountable for anything that turns out negative. Whatever your enterprise, stick with the principle of total accountability and the dividends will eventually pay off in a very big way.

People who lack accountability in business are more dangerous than common thieves who break into your office and steal you blind. At least with thieves, you can buy an insurance plan to cover your losses after the robbery. But people who lack *accountability* also lack introspection and often rationalize their bad behavior. If they leave you hanging for their debt, they say, "Well, that's just business." If you work with too many clients who refuse to pay their debts on time, it can put your small business in serious danger. Nothing has hurt my business more than working with organizations and people who were not accountable for their actions. When I have extended credit to organizations that haven't paid me, it has always been my company that suffered the consequences.

The best and most successful business people are those who know how to turn their failures into successes. I recently had dinner with some friends at Zoe's, a downtown Seattle restaurant. I had never been to this restaurant before, but I had heard very good reviews about it. When my party arrived at the restaurant, it was packed. We had reservations, so we were seated on time, and we all ordered cocktails. After a few minutes, the waitress informed us that the bar was backed up and that our cocktails were not ready. She apologized and asked us to pick out two hors d'oeurves from the menu, saying they would be on the house.

This waitress immediately turned what could have been a possible negative into a strong positive experience. When the hors d'oeurves and the main course did arrive, the food was outstanding. I wasn't surprised at all.

This kind of accountability is not often found in business. But as you can see, taking responsibility for your actions when things go wrong *does* pay off. People will respect you for admitting your mistakes. If you can find a way to turn those mistakes around and provide your clients with improved service, that's even better! Your clients will come back to you if they know you care enough about them to make up for your mistakes. I will definitely be recommending Zoe's Restaurant to my friends for their good food and excellent service.

CHAPTER EIGHT

Option Thinking

"A person's greatest triumph is to achieve stability and regale in a world of shifting threats and terrifying challenges."

—Bertrand Russell

A necessary skill for the self-employed business owner is *option thinking*—that is, the ability to consider *multiple* options. This skill can help you in making decisions, handling setbacks, correcting mistakes, and expanding your business. Option thinking means examining all of your options before making a decision, and also means being open to new possibilities.

The type of option thinking you do will depend on your business. It may mean choosing to offer several different types of services to your clients. It may mean choosing to seek out a different type of potential client, who may be more receptive to your business than the clients you are currently dealing with. It may mean changing your business model to one that may be more successful. As a business owner, you must keep an open mind. Those who are *flexible* and who can adapt easily to change have a much better chance of succeeding in business.

Again, when I first started my own business, I published a newspaper aimed at the older population. Later, I hosted a radio show aimed at this same target audience, featuring clients that were advertising in my newspaper as my radio sponsors. I did not consider myself to be in the media buying business at this point, even though I was purchasing radio air time for my newspaper clients *outside* of the time period of my thirty-minute radio show. I saw the media buying as supplemental to my newspaper.

Then one day, I got a call from a sales manager at a software company. "I need to buy some air time for radio commercials. Do you do media buying, Mr. Casey?"

I had about two seconds to answer this question. So I said, "Yes, I do."

"Great," said the sales manager. "I'd like to do business with you."

This turned out to be the biggest boost to my business ever. Soon I was doing media buying for numerous clients outside of my newspaper advertisers and making much more income than I was with my radio show. And all because I was flexible enough to consider a new option for doing business. If I'd had a different answer when the software sales manager called me (e.g., "No, not really. I only do occasional media buying for the clients who are advertising in my newspaper."), I would have missed out on a valuable opportunity, and my business would be very different today.

BREAKING WITH TRADITION

Of course, this kind of flexibility goes against "traditional" business thinking. For most of the 20th century, we've been taught that a "nose to the grindstone" mentality is the key element for achieving success. It used to be that we were born, went to school, got a job, worked for the same company for forty years, and retired. During that time, most of us also got married and had children.

Now after we finish school, we might work for seven different companies and go back to school several more times before retiring. After retiring, some of us choose to go back to work. Our home life is often just as unpredictable. We may get married, have children, then divorce, get married again, and have more children. Our children from our first marriage may move back home. (Hopefully, they move out again very quickly.) We may take care of our aging parents—and so on.

In an ever-changing world, the key to success today is more about being alert to new opportunities. You must keep your eyes and ears open at all times for new options that can benefit your life and your business. Again, this is why I think it's best not to get too hung up in the "how to" of creating a business, simply because there is no one "right way" to do it. A linear five- to ten-year business plan may have been useful forty years ago, but it is *not* the model you want to use today. Success in business is no longer about getting from Point A to Point B. It's about getting from Point A to Point D, back to Point C, and over to Point Q.

Modern business practice more closely resembles a circle of events that a straight line. I can almost guarantee that whatever type of business you start today, it will be very different five years from now. Your business will change over time as you adopt new perspectives, take on new clients, offer new products or services, and possibly even expand into new fields or industries. Nothing I am doing today, including writing this book, is what I was doing five years ago.

MAKING ADJUSTMENTS

As a business owner, you must be flexible enough to make *adjustments* when your business doesn't work in quite the way that you thought it would. For example, say you open a restaurant in what you think is a prime location. You are near an office park, and you expect to get a lot of business from the "after work" crowd. As such, you have created a menu featuring mid-priced entrees (e.g., chicken parmesan, shrimp alfredo, barbecued spare ribs) that might appeal to young professionals who would like to enjoy a quiet dinner after a hard day's work.

But once you open your doors, you discover a problem. Most people who work in the office park go home to their families after five o'clock. They rarely stop at your restaurant after work, except on Friday nights—and, of course, on Saturday and Sundays, the last place they will come is near their work place.

It is here that many businesses start to die. In the case of restaurants, sometimes the owner is also the chef, and the chef is too proud of their food to make the necessary adjustments to keep the business going. If the clientele doesn't respond to the cuisine, the chef blames the customers for the lack of business. "These people just don't appreciate good food!"

Those who can adapt will succeed.

An Option Thinker will find a way to make the business work using a different strategy. As the restaurant owner, you might decide to close the restaurant at night, but to open it for breakfast and lunch. Or you might start a catering business that serves the office park and others like it. Or, if you look around and discover that most of your clients are not young professionals, but students from the small college down the street, you might adjust your menu to serve entrées (e.g., cheeseburger baskets, chicken fingers, fried onions, and mozzarella sticks) that would appeal to college students. Five years later, your business will still be going strong, but it will be a very different restaurant from what you first envisioned it would be.

Those who can adapt will succeed.

STAYING FOCUSED

Making adjustments to your business can be a slippery slope. The ability to stay focused is a critical element in building a successful business and keeping it going. There is a subtle difference between being flexible and being all over the map. When I say that my business is not the same today as it was five years ago, I mean that many of my clients are different, and my role as CEO of my company has changed. But I am still in the marketing and communications business.

When I made the transition from publishing my newspaper to selling radio air time, it was a gradual transition. As I said, I had been doing media buying for the advertising clients in my newspaper for a while before I started doing it for other clients. Also, a lot of the day-to-day aspects of my newspaper business, such as sales calls to potential clients, planning ad campaigns, carried over into my new media buying business. Basically, when my newspaper wasn't as successful as I'd originally thought, I moved from one type of communications business to another.

When you are struggling in business, there is always a tendency to depart from your core plan. There is a difference between making adjustments to improve your business and making a sudden "wildcat" move into a business that you know nothing about. Let's go back to the restaurant example. You have just opened your restaurant, but the evening customer base is not as strong as you expected.

This is the time when you are most at risk to step out and make a fatal mistake. Instead of making adjustments to improve the business, you might decide to go in a completely different direction. You might see an empty storefront across the street, and decide to open up a laundromat because someone once told you that it was easy money. Or you might decide to try one of those "Make $100,000 in sixty days selling time-sharing condos in Zimbabwe" easy-money schemes.

Instead of making an unwise move that takes you away from the business you've started, you need to stay focused, add value to your product or service, or make adjustments to allow your business to work in a different way. At times like this, it's a good idea to review the five reasons that you came up with in Chapter One for wanting to own your own business. Reviewing these reasons will remind you of your goals and objectives for your business, and will help to keep you on track in your efforts to fulfill those goals and objectives.

A CASE STUDY—UPHOLSTERY INC.

My brother owns an upholstery business, Upholstery Inc. He started out as an assistant in an upholstery shop, learned the skills of the trade, and eventually graduated to being a full-time upholsterer. After working in the business for several years, he decided to open his own upholstery shop, offering services to homeowners who wanted their sofas and chairs reupholstered with new fabric.

Unfortunately, while he loved the work, his original business model wasn't very practical for making money. When he received a call from a prospective client, he would often have to drive across town to meet with them, hauling a dozen or so fabric sample books with him so that the client would have a wide variety of samples to choose from. Sometimes it would take hours for the client to decide on which fabric they wanted—and sometimes, after examining all the sample books, they would decide that they really didn't want to have their sofa or chair reupholstered after all!

If they did decide to use his upholstery service, my brother would have return to their house a few days later with a rented truck and haul the sofa or chair back across town to his shop. He then had to order the fabric for the job. It sometimes took several weeks for special fabric orders to be delivered. During this time, his client would often call every few days to ask how the job was going, when it would be finished, etc.

When he finished the job, my brother would then have to haul the sofa back across town to the client's house. And here, his troubles were just beginning. Sometimes, the client was not happy with the fabric that they themselves had selected for the job. There was nothing wrong with the quality of my brother's work. But the client's original vision of what the sofa or chair would look like with a particular fabric design did not match what the sofa or chair actually looked like after the work was finished. Since these sofas or chairs were sometimes priceless family heirlooms, the client would insist that the job be done over with a different type of fabric.

My brother has a passion for upholstery; he considers it to be his own special area of creative expertise. He did not want to lose his business, so he made adjustments to his business model that would allow him to make more money with fewer hassles.

He started to pursue a different kind of clientele. His new customers included hotels and motels, banks, franchise restaurants, hospitals, theaters, and other businesses with high-volume upholstering needs. Pursuing these types of customers allowed him to significantly reduce his overhead costs. The skill level needed to repair restaurant booths and theater seats is not as high as that for custom upholstery work, so he had a larger pool of potential employees to choose from. Also, the upholstery materials for these jobs is not as expensive and could be ordered and delivered from his suppliers in a few days, rather than a few weeks.

Once his business started to take off with high-volume and *repetitive* upholstery work, my brother purchased a large used trailer to haul around his equipment. This enabled him to actually do the upholstery work *on site!* He no longer had to haul chairs and sofas back and forth across town in order to do a job. The trailer also provided him with the mobility to take jobs in other cities. He has since taken his trailer up and down the West Coast, doing jobs for multiple businesses.

The moral of this story, once again, is that flexibility and the ability to adapt and change are essential for business survival. My brother would probably not be in business today if he hadn't been willing to make the necessary adjustments to make his business more profitable and less troublesome.

ANTICIPATING SETBACKS

It is an absolute certainty, in life and in business, that no matter what you do, you will encounter setbacks. If you don't, it means you are playing it too safe. Fortunately, with a bit of strategic option thinking, you can learn how to anticipate setbacks, how to plan for them, and how to overcome them.

The kinds of setbacks that you encounter in your business will, of course, depend on the kind of business you have. Many businesses fail because their owners don't take the possibility of failure into account. "We've got such a perfect product/service/ business plan, there's *no way* we can fail," they say to themselves. Unfortunately, once they start their business, they often encounter setbacks that they never anticipated—because they never *tried* to anticipate them.

The wise thing to do is to look ahead and ask yourself, "What kinds of potential setbacks could I encounter with my product or service? Can I avoid some of these setbacks? If I can't avoid them, how can I get past them?"

Look at your product or service, your potential customer, and your business strategy and ask yourself, "What *could* go wrong here? What are the potential problems that my business could encounter?" Often, this is a matter of good market research, of making an accurate assessment of your own skills and business resources, and of understanding your potential customer's attitude towards your product or service.

Of course, you don't want to overlook anything. Be careful of saying to yourself, "Naah, there's no way *this* or *that* could be a problem in the future." Take special care to look at those areas of your business where you *don't* anticipate setbacks. Are there potential hazards lurking in these areas? Remember that, many times, setbacks come from the area of business that we were *sure* would give us no trouble.

Anticipating setbacks is hard to do when you're just starting your own business. After all, you've never been here before. Again, it's a good idea to talk to someone with experience, someone who *has* been here before. Talk to your competitors or to people who have businesses similar to yours, and to other small business owners. Find out what kinds of setbacks they've encountered in starting their business and how they got past them. You can learn a great deal about what to anticipate and what to avoid by listening to the "war stories" of those who have fought their way through business battles before you. As you gain more experience as a self-employed business owner, it will be easier for you to look ahead and see the setbacks that your business might encounter.

PROBLEM-SOLVING

Of course, you can't anticipate or avoid *every* setback. There are always day-to-day problems that arise in every business. But these can be dealt with using option thinking as well. When you encounter problems or setbacks in your business, try to deal with them on an *incremental level*. Often, large problems are made up of smaller problems. Try to fix the smaller problems one by one, rather than trying to fix the entire problem all at once. In business, it is more important to pay attention to the small details while keeping the "big picture" in the back of your mind.

We can learn a lesson here from the great quarterbacks of football, such as Johnny Unitas, Curt Warner, and Joe Montana. When they suffer a setback in a football game, they ask themselves: "How do I get myself and my team out of our current circumstance?"

An important characteristic of a good quarterback is the ability to focus on the "here and now." If their team suffers a setback in the middle of a game (e.g., if the other team has just scored a touchdown on a recovered fumble), the quarterback has the ability to literally shake off the loss and deal with the present. This is called *incremental thinking*—thinking in increments or in terms of the next small problem to be overcome, rather than trying to fix the overall big problem all at once.

In the case of the quarterback, they focus on the next play, rather than thinking about what the score will be at the end of the game or about the playoff game that will be played several weeks from now. If the team doesn't win this game, the upcoming playoff game won't mean anything.

Sometimes the quarterback must take a short loss in order to get the game back on track. The good quarterback knows it's better not to panic and try a high-risk move at the first sign of trouble. Scrambling around deeper in the pocket and trying frantically to make something happen will, more often than not, result in a much bigger loss, a fumble, or an interception.

Usually, however, the quarterback has anticipated the current setback and has already thought of a plan to get out of it. When he runs a play, he doesn't have just one player in mind to pass or hand-off to as he goes back into the pocket. He has several target players in mind to choose from. When the quarterback hikes the ball, he will look around to see who is open, and who has the best chance of catching the ball and carrying it for some distance down the field. This is the essence of option thinking.

When you encounter problems in your business, remember to focus on the "here and now," rather than what is to come in the future. Fixing the bugs in your own product or service, or providing better service to your current clients should be more important than landing that huge account with a major corporation. If you don't have time to handle the problems of all your current clients, it may be that you're trying to do too much at once and it is time to scale back your operations. Sometimes you must be willing to take a loss—whether it is a financial loss and/or the loss of a potential client—in order to get your business back on track.

Always remember to take a close look at *ALL* the options you have for fixing your problems or setbacks. There is usually more than one solution to any given problem. When you examine *ALL* your options, it's easier to decide which solution will be the most effective. If you can't find an adequate solution, or you are unsure of which solution to take, remember this: Unlike the quarterback (who can't stop in the middle of a play and ask his teammates for advice), *you* have the option of asking for help. If you ask your clients and your peers for advice on what *they* think would be the best solution to a problem, they can often point you in the right direction and sometimes even suggest solutions that you might not have thought of.

THE CUSTOMER IS *NOT* ALWAYS RIGHT

You've often heard the expression, "The customer is always right." This sounds like a noble goal, but the self-employed business owner should be aware that it's simply not true.

The maxim of "The customer is always right" was created primarily for the restaurant and retail industries—and it is in these industries that this maxim works best. The idea behind the maxim is that customer service is top priority and customers *must* be satisfied. Therefore, if a restaurant customer doesn't like their meal, the waiter should allow them to select a new entrée. If a customer buys a dress and then wants to return it because she suddenly decides that she doesn't like the color, she must be allowed to do so. Even when the customer is wrong, they are "always right."

If you plan to open a restaurant or a retail store, it will benefit your business to follow this maxim most of the time. Certainly, you will get a lot of repeat business if you go out of your way to satisfy your customers, even when they are not satisfied.

For most self-employed business owners, however, the maxim of "the customer is always right" should be taken with a grain of salt. Of course, you should always try to do the best job possible and satisfy your clients in every way. If a client has a reasonable complaint, you should address it immediately, and make corrections so that the client is satisfied. If the client has a certain way that they want something done (e.g., "We *must* include this concept in our marketing campaign."), you must be flexible and creative enough to accommodate them as much as possible. Always make sure that the client gets the best product or service that you can give. But the simple fact is, the customer is *not* always right.

I would estimate that about 80 percent of the people I encounter are a pleasure to work with in business. 10 percent are indifferent, and the other 10 percent are "high maintenance" clients. It is this last 10 percent that you need to be aware of.

High-maintenance clients are the customers that *think* they are always right—but seldom are. They are never satisfied with your product or service. They don't trust you to do the job that they hired you for, because they believe that *they* can do it better. They insist on doing things "their way," even when you suggest that doing things another way might be more effective. And they question the cost and necessity of everything you do for them.

Your best strategy is to simply avoid working with such clients. Trust me, you will save yourself plenty of mental and financial frustration if you do not work with high-maintenance business people. It may be hard for you to turn down these clients when you are just starting out and need the business. Sometimes, it seems as if you must take on the "devil's client" to get the money you need for next month's rent.

Again, one of my major reasons for owning my own business is freedom of association. I want the freedom to choose which clients I will work with, and which clients I will turn down. I have to say, it's a pleasure to work with the 80 percent of people who are *not* "high-maintenance." Most people *want* you to succeed and will help you to succeed, especially if you are doing business with them. Seek those people out and avoid the rest as much as you can.

The key to long-term success is not the money, but rising to a level where you can choose the clients you want to work with.

THE TAKERS

I have a special name for the "high-maintenance" business people you should make every effort to avoid as clients. I call them "The Takers." It takes a bit of skill to be able to recognize these types, but in general, they have some common characteristics that make them easy to spot:

1. They are the most demanding clients. They can't really articulate what they want in a product or service, but whatever you are doing for them, you are doing it wrong.

2. They want to pay the least amount of money for the job. They try to grind you down on your price or even squeeze you for the money. They think they are being smart and thrifty, but actually their behavior is boorish and it eventually costs them.

3. They see themselves as being first in everything. Everyone else is second.

Unfortunately, some Takers may not be quite so obvious. You may actually like them, and turning them down may be difficult because you would really like to do business with them. But underneath their rosy exterior is a person who has developed some bad habits. Many Takers are time-wasters. They forget appointments, or they are constantly running late, or they don't respond to you in a timely manner. Time is your most precious commodity, and using it wisely helps you to beat out the competition. You can't afford to be around people who are Takers or time wasters.

You will find that people who run late are *always* running late. People who keep you waiting will *always* keep you waiting. It really doesn't matter what the excuse is. Most of the time, the excuse appears valid but the end result is the same. These people are wasting your time. You must develop the mindset early on that time is money and your time is extremely valuable.

I have a close relationship with one associate that dates back twenty years. He is a very likeable person and is very competent. Ever since I have known him, however, he has been disorganized and is always running late. For many years, he has struggled to keep his accounting business going. I know that one major reason he has such a difficult time with his business is that he often shows up late for appointments or sometimes even forgets appointments altogether. I have tried to tell him about this, but he just doesn't seem to make the connection. His life always seems to be so chaotic. He is continually doing too many projects at once and always seems to be flying by the seat of his pants.

I have a confession to make. I used to be chronically late myself. I seldom had trouble being on time for business appointments, but I was consistently late for personal appointments. I had every excuse in the book. I would justify it to myself by saying, "I am working for myself so I deserve a little slack," or "Don't sweat it. They'll understand."

Then one day, I woke up and changed my mindset. I decided that it was no longer acceptable for me to run late for *any* appointment. I have since done everything in my power to be on time for all my appointments, personal or business. On those rare occasions when I am running late, I always call the party on my cell phone and let them know, even if I will only be five minutes late.

When you are on time for your appointments, every other aspect of your life improves as well. You are much calmer because you don't have to drive as fast. The most important factor, however, is that by being on time, you make a statement to the other person that you consider their time to be as valuable as yours.

I will wait for an appointment a maximum of fifteen minutes. In the early years, when I really needed the business, I would wait longer. Now, after fifteen minutes, I hand a card to the receptionist in the waiting room and politely ask them to tell the person I was supposed to meet with to call me when they would like to reschedule the appointment. You must demonstrate to a potential client that your time is valuable too. If handled properly, they will respect you for it. Usually, when someone has missed an appointment with me, they will immediately call me to reschedule it and apologize for having missed me.

TROUBLE AHEAD

One of the most important skills you can develop as a self-employed business person is the skill of knowing when it's time to walk away. When your gut instinct tells you that something is not right with a client, it is better to turn them down than to learn the hard way that they are dishonest or a bad business person.

I recently turned down a potential client whom I had been cultivating for some time. I originally approached this client because I had purchased the company's product and was very satisfied with the results. I called the marketing director of the company to offer my radio advertising services. The marketing director agreed to meet with me, saying that his company's recent radio campaigns hadn't been very effective.

I developed some strong messaging concepts and radio placement ideas I thought would help the company. When I met with the marketing director, I could tell he was interested in my ideas and wanted to pursue them further. Then he asked if I knew the media buyer his company normally used to place radio campaigns. I hadn't met this person, but agreed to meet with her. The last thing I want to do is ace anyone out of their commission.

I met with the media buyer and provided her with the details of what I was planning with her client. She told me she had no problem with the concepts I had developed and that my working with her client would not interfere with her contract with them. The next day, the marketing director called and requested that I meet with the company president to get his approval for the project. Again, he said that he wanted his existing media buyer to be included in the process. I called the media buyer and invited her to the meeting. She said she would do her best to attend and thanked me for keeping her so well-informed.

But when I met with the company president, the media buyer was not there. The company president approved my plan for the radio campaign, and I returned to my office thinking that I had just landed a valuable client. But a few days later, I received an e-mail from the marketing director. After our meeting, he had sent an e-mail with the specifics of my plan to the existing media buyer. She had sent him a reply in which she had ripped my plan apart. The marketing director had then forwarded her reply on to me.

I was very angry the media buyer had not been honest with me and that she had sandbagged the proposal behind my back. I was also not happy the marketing director had shared her criticizing e-mail with me. It seemed as if the client was trying to play us off one another. When the marketing director called me back to offer suggestions for some creative aspects of the radio campaign, I told him that I had decided not to work with his company.

Again, the quicker you can spot clients who might give you trouble, the easier it is to avoid that trouble by turning them down. Your goal should be to establish long-term relationships with clients you can trust. If you find you cannot trust the people you work for, it is better to simply not work with them.

As William Gladstone once said, *"Choose wisely your companions, for a young man's companions, more than food or clothing, his home, or his parents, make him what he is."*

ACTIONS SPEAK LOUDER THAN WORDS

If a coach breaks a contract with a college athletic department and leaps to another institution for a huge amount of money, many people seem to be indifferent about it. I hear people say, "*Anyone* would do what he did." This is *so* not true. I know of plenty of coaches who believe that teaching is their primary mission. They realize that if they abandon their contract, they will abandon their commitment to the athletes, to the students they have recruited. They know that if they walk away from their word, they are making a huge lifestyle statement to the young people that they coach.

I used to hear that executives would play golf with a prospective executive recruit before they even considered hiring that person. When I first heard about this, I assumed that the boss was trying to show the recruit how great their life could be if they worked hard. I found out otherwise when I started playing golf in my late twenties. Golf is a game of honor. You keep your own score, and therefore it is easy to shade a few strokes. Anyone who plays the game will tell you how frustrating it can be. A really good shot can be quickly wiped out by a bad shot.

An executive or business owner can learn a lot about potential recruits, business partners, and possible future associates during a four-hour round of golf. You can find out if they are honest. Do they keep their score accurately? You can learn about their temperament. Can they control their temper, or do they pitch their nine-iron into the lake after making a bad shot? You can also learn about how they deal with setbacks. After making that bad shot, can they concentrate on making the *next* one? Between holes, you find out how they think about things outside the workplace and what is important to them. In golf, you can learn a lot about people outside the business environment.

I'm not suggesting that you should necessarily take all your potential business associates out for a round of golf, but you should observe how your associates and potential clients think and act while doing business with you. Actions speak louder than words. Observing how someone makes an ethical choice or reacts in a situation will tell you if that person is someone you should do business with or associate with. What a person does will often give you more insight into their true character than what they say.

COMPETITORS ARE YOUR BEST FRIENDS

Competitors are your best friends. They validate what you are doing and keep you sharp and on top of your game. I know this concept is almost impossible to fathom now, but if you were the only accountant in the world, potential customers would have a hard time understanding why they would need your services. In all likelihood, they would be happy doing their own accounting because there wouldn't be a precedent established to do it any other way.

If you are thinking of opening your own accounting firm, you will have an easier time marketing your services because of all the successful accounting firms that have come before you. These firms have already have laid a foundation for you to build on. This doesn't mean that every business will want to use *your* accounting service, but at least the average business owner understands the advantages of having an accountant. If you fail, don't blame your competitors.

When I first started my business, I believed that my newspaper for older adults was an innovation. The older adult market had long been ignored in news publishing, and I thought I could change that. Of course, I didn't have to convince potential advertisers that *newspapers* were a valid medium for reaching their markets. *The New York Times*, *The Wall Street Journal*, and the millions of other newspapers that have been in circulation around the globe for centuries had already done that for me.

I did, however, have a problem in communicating my vision for my *own* newspaper to my potential advertisers. My core advertising targets included travel agencies, retirement centers, financial institutions, estate-planning attorneys, bookstores, health care facilities, and technology companies that catered to the older population. My publication was targeted to a very specific demographic that made up the clientele for these businesses. From my point of view, there was no reason why they *shouldn't* want to advertise in my newspaper!

I have since learned that these businesses did not trust my newspaper because it was so new. The concept of a newspaper that was published specifically for an older population had never been successfully tested before. Many of my advertising targets turned me down because they were unwilling to commit their marketing budgets to a brand new newspaper that was still trying to build its audience.

"No, we'll just stick with the daily newspaper for now" was a response I often heard. Advertisers were more willing to trust a newspaper like the *Seattle Times,* which has been in circulation for over a hundred years and has a well-established readership. Another typical response was "Older people are very set in their ways. They're not going to look around for a new newspaper to read."

To top it off, I learned that two other publications aimed at the older adult market were starting up in Seattle at the very same time I began publishing my newspaper. One was based locally and was very similar to my operation. The other publication was based out of state. Now there would be *three* newspapers going after the same local market and potential advertisers. *There just isn't room in this town for three of us!* I thought.

I was almost ready to throw in the towel. But being a stubborn person, I kept pushing. Soon, I was selling enough ads to cover the cost of the newspaper. The other publications targeting older adults were going after the same advertisers. They would win a few and I would win a few. I often looked at the ads in their publications and thought bitterly of all the advertisers I could have had in my paper if it weren't for them.

But over time, I slowly realized that my competitors were actually *validating* what I was trying to do. The presence of *three* newspapers for the older adult market started to convince the local business community that this market was important and it was essential to have publications that catered to the needs of older adults. I began looking at my competitors in a totally different way.

I enthusiastically perused their publications for editorial ideas and possible advertisers. After reading one of my competitor's newspapers, I would often say to myself, "I never would have thought of going after *that* type of advertiser—but I will now!"

I also realized that, when all was said and done, I needed about thirty-five to forty ads in an average issue to make a pretty good living. Since there were *thousands* of potential advertisers in the area, the last thing I needed to worry about was my competitors stealing my business.

I soon became the cheering section for my competitors. I hoped that their publications would succeed and that their readers would respond well to their advertising. When I called on a potential client that had had a good experience in a competitor's publication, my sales pitch became a lot easier. My competitors and I all did little things to try to gain a competitive edge. In doing so, we all became stronger publications.

I was the first to feature color photos in my newspaper. The other publications soon followed. One of my competitors had a strong local editorial content. I followed his example and added the same type of content to my newspaper.

One of the publications died within a couple of years because of high overhead. I knew they were selling about the same amount of advertising I was, but I could also see that they were spending too much money on expensive office space and a large staff. They had an editor, photographer, sales manager, graphics artist, layout person, and a few more employees. I had a staff of one person. Me! This publication was also from out of state, and I think this hurt them a bit, since they could only provide their readership with an out-of-state perspective on local events and concerns.

I wasn't sorry to see this publication go, because most of their advertisers did not have a good experience with them. The other publication was locally owned, and the publisher, like me, kept his overhead expenses low. But even though one of these publications ultimately failed, my competitors and I still established a precedent. Together, we proved that there was a market for newspapers aimed at the older population. For the *niche market* publications that follow us, it will be much easier to prove to potential clients the value of advertising in such publications. They can point to our example and say, "Look! These fellows did it! So can we!"

BUILD CLIENTS…NOT CUSTOMERS

One of the basic principles of succeeding in business is to approach each client or customer with the intent of developing a long-term relationship. If you are an accountant or lawyer, you usually refer to your base as "clients." If you own a restaurant or are in the retail business, you usually refer to your base as "customers." The lawyers and accountants have it right! A client is about establishing a long-term relationship. A customer is someone who walks into an establishment, buys an item, and walks out. You may or may not ever see them again.

When you go to a restaurant for a meal, do you feel like a customer or a client? In most of the restaurants I visit, I feel like a customer. I am satisfied with the meal, but I don't feel very special. Overall, I've had a good experience, but one that could be made even better.

The best strategy for any business that regularly services customers is to try to turn them into clients. You do this by offering good food, a superior choice of products, exceptional service, a friendly atmosphere, or whatever it takes to make customers *want to return* to your business. If you can provide your customers with an excellent experience, if you can make them *remember* you in a favorable light, they will keep coming back to your business for more of the same.

If the espresso cart owner who stands outside the community college views the students and faculty there as clients—if they provide great espresso service, friendly conversation, and even call their clients by their first names—those clients will keep coming back to that espresso cart for as long as they attend the college. If an airline ever decides to treat all of its passengers (not just those in first class) as clients, with comfortable seats, polite service, and food that is actually edible, it may find itself overwhelmed by the number of people clamoring to fly with them.

SUCCESS MEANS RAISING EXPECTATIONS

Many years ago, I interviewed Robin Leach, host of the TV show, *Lifestyles of the Rich and Famous*. At the time I interviewed him, his show was at the height of its popularity. I asked him how it felt to have really made it to the top. From the expression on his face, I could tell that he was irritated by my question. I now understand why. He said that he was just like any other working stiff who got up day after day to slug it out. He spoke of six-day workweeks and of trying to consistently put together a quality show.

What Robin Leach was trying to tell me is that you never really make it. There is never that moment where you look down from the ivory tower and say, "I have arrived!" As soon as Robin Leach put one show to bed, he was working on the next show. *Lifestyles of the Rich and Famous* has long since been cancelled. I don't know what Robin Leach is doing now, but I am sure that he is trying to figure out his next gig.

Success is all about raising expectations. After you have succeeded with one project, your client will expect the same, or perhaps a higher level of quality in your product or service the next time around. You will be judged only by what you do with your next project, your next event, your next magazine article, your next software program, your next dinner, your next presentation, your next book, your next movie, your next radio spot, your next at bat, or your next concert. With each successful project, you establish a new standard for future expectations.

> **With each successful project, you establish a new standard for future expectations.**

This is why establishing consistency is an absolute key to your overall success. One reason McDonald's has been so successful is because of the consistency of its product and service. If you walk into a McDonald's in Portland, Oregon, or Portland, Maine, the Big Mac will taste exactly the same. McDonald's was the first commercial restaurant to recognize that convenience and consistency of service are more important to success than the quality of the food. A Big Mac is not the best-tasting burger, but with McDonald's fast-food process, it can be made consistently and served to the customers in a matter of minutes. This is very important to people who want to enjoy a quick lunch and don't want to wait around for their food, as they might have to do at a fancier restaurant.

Consistency of product or service is important no matter what type of business you are in, simply because one failure may be enough to kill your relationship with any client. If you run a laundromat, you must do a great job of cleaning the client's shirts every time. If you fail, you will not be remembered for the dozens of spotlessly clean shirts you returned to that client, but for the one shirt that was shrunk to the size of a handker-chief because you left it in the steamer too long. If you are a tax accountant, you will not be remembered for having saved your client thousands of dollars in tax deductions through the years, but for the one tax form you forgot to file that resulted in an IRS audit for your client.

Of course, the easiest way to achieve consistency is to make a point of showing up and doing a good job for each client you serve. When a restaurant closes its doors at the end of each night, the owner is already thinking about how to serve his customers the next day. A good tax accountant is already thinking about the deductions and extra money-saving services that his clients will need over the next quarter and the next fiscal year. When you are a self-employed business owner, taking a look ahead at the start of each new project will often suggest new ways that you can provide your clients with products or services to match the quality of your last project.

KNOW WHEN TO SAY "NO"

In business, you have to make tough calls. I believe that many people don't go into business for themselves because they have a problem with saying the word "No." To succeed in business, you must be firm and direct. This means you must know when to turn someone down.

Some "No's" are easy, such as when you get a call asking if you'd like to change your long-distance service. Unless you are one of those rare people in the world who is actually *looking* for a better long-distance service, simply say "Thank you. I'm not interested" and hang up. If you are offered a scheme that prom-ises to make $100,000 in six months, you would be smart to turn it down. Again, if it seems too good to be true, it probably is.

Other "No's" may be a bit more difficult. If you sense that a client is a "Taker," or that they will be difficult to work with, or that something about them is not quite honest, it can be very hard to turn them down, especially if you need the business. If you sense that the client does not really need your services, it can be hard to refuse them if you know that working with them would be very profitable. But it is better to be honest than to lead them on the business equivalent of a wild goose chase, making them spend money for business services that they don't really need. They will respect you more if you tell them the truth, and they will almost always come back to you when the time comes that they really *do* need your services.

If you are someone who has a problem with saying "No," you might want to reconsider going into business for yourself. Saying "No" is being tough when you have to. It is a skill that can be practiced, but it can't really be learned.

ACT DECISIVELY

Bruce Nordstrom, CEO of Nordstrom, Inc., taught me a valuable lesson in business long before I even considered going into business for myself. In the late 1970's, Mr. Nordstrom served as a volunteer and advisor on a task force that was seeking a transit solution for downtown Seattle. At the time, I was the Public Affairs Director for the project. I was providing staff support for this task force. I noticed some significant things about the way that Mr. Nordstrom communicated with other people.

> **He always answered the phone in person.**

First, when he was in his office, Mr. Nordstrom never used an administrative assistant or secretary to screen his calls. He always answered the phone in person. If I called to ask if he would consider chairing a new transportation committee or if he would do an interview with a Seattle newspaper about the challenges of transportation facing our region, he wouldn't keep me waiting for my answer. He never said to me, "Well, I don't know. Why don't you call me next week, and I'll let you know if I can do it."

After I made my pitch, he would pause for about five seconds and give me his answer. "No, I can't chair that task force at this time." Or "Yes I can do the interview. Set it up for this time next week." Our conversations generally lasted thirty seconds or less. He didn't waste his time or mine floundering about. He knew instantly whether he had the time, knowledge, or desire to proceed with my request. When he was asked a question he acted *decisively.*

This is a great lesson, and one that is imperative if you wish to start a successful business. With each successful project, you establish a new standard for future expectations.

CHAPTER NINE

The Personality Factor

What do Presidents Eisenhower, Kennedy, Reagan, Clinton, and George W. Bush all have in common? What do Presidents Johnson, Nixon, Carter, and George H. W. Bush all have in common? The first group of presidents were and are generally well-liked because they had personalities that connected well with the American public. The second group of presidents did not have personalities that connected well with the American people when they were in office.

All of the presidents I've mentioned here had a major setback or at least one major crisis that they didn't handle particularly well. Eisenhower survived two heart attacks while in office, and there were questions as to whether or not he could continue on as president. Kennedy had the Bay of Pigs debacle, Reagan the Iran-Contra affair, and Clinton the Monica Lewinsky scandal.

In contrast, Johnson didn't survive the politics of Vietnam, Nixon fell to Watergate, Carter couldn't move beyond the Iran hostage crisis, and George H. W. Bush, after stopping the Persian Gulf War just short of a complete victory over Iraq, was faced with a recession in the United States. Many people felt that his economic policies were insufficient to pull the country out of the recession and that Bush himself was out of touch with the needs of the American people.

The presidents who had a personality that connected well with the average American survived, and sometimes even prospered, under crisis conditions. The others were either one-term presidents or, in Nixon's case, forced to resign. (As of this writing, George W. Bush faces some major challenges as he grapples with Iraq and the national economy, but his popularity remains high. Having a personality that connects well with people is not a guarantee that anyone will win reelection, but it is a major factor and may make the difference between winning and losing.)

The same can be said of self-employment. If you have a personality that connects well with other people, you have a better chance of succeeding in business. Are you someone who communicates well with others? Do you project confidence in your own abilities, a confidence that enables people to trust you? Are you able to work well with other people and to recognize their point of view? If so, your chances of success in business are that much greater.

The good news is that even if you don't have a "bubbling personality" and are somewhat uncomfortable being around other people, you can still succeed in business. Competence in your product or services still goes a long way towards success. There are numerous examples of people who are not well-liked, but who have still been highly-successful in starting their own business. But it makes your job much easier if you can connect and relate to people.

It also helps to have a good sense of humor. Again, I can't say that you won't succeed in business without humor. I have seen people succeed whose sense of humor was similar to wet paint. But when things go wrong or get sticky, the ability to see the lighter side of a situation can help you to make it through the rough times.

Other elements of your personality can have a significant impact on your business as well. Again, there is no one "right personality" for the self-employed business owner. But it is a good idea for you to be aware of these personality elements and of the positive and negative ways they can affect you.

SELF-CONFIDENCE: YES/ ARROGANCE: NO

If you own a business, self-confidence is not an option; it's an absolute must! You must be confident about yourself as a person and demonstrate that confidence to others. You can't expect other people to follow your lead if you yourself don't believe strongly in your own skills and in your product or service.

But there is a fine line between confidence and arrogance. Arrogance is the quality of being *too* confident, of believing that no client can do without your product or service and that *you* are the only person in the world who can provide them with it. Like confidence, people pick up on arrogance very quickly. If a client senses that you are patronizing them, or if you treat them as if they are not intelligent enough to understand the benefits of your product or service, it is very easy for them to turn you down. Usually, they give you a standard excuse (e.g., "We just don't have the budget for this."), but they never tell you the *real* reason why they are refusing you.

Arrogance is also assuming that your business is going to succeed and not having a backup plan in case something goes wrong. Again, if you think you have an absolute, can't-miss, guaranteed business, it might be a good idea to stop and think about what *could* conceivably go wrong with it. Pay special attention if you find yourself examining a potential problem and saying, "That could *never* happen." Disasters and setbacks often come from the places we least expect. Chances are, what you think could never happen, can and *will* happen.

Remember the lesson of the Titanic. There weren't enough lifeboats for all the passengers on the ship, because the ship itself was thought to be "unsinkable." When the ship actually *did* sink after hitting an iceberg, the lack of lifeboats resulted in a huge, catastrophic loss of life. Don't let the risks of business overwhelm you, but don't underestimate them either. You cannot *eliminate* risk; you can only minimize your exposure to it. Always hope for the best, but be prepared for the worst.

ADVERSITY

How do you handle adversity? Are you able to keep going when things go bad, not just in business, but in your personal life as well? Do you have the emotional capacity to handle a personal trauma and run a business at the same time?

I mention this because I have actually seen businesses close when the owners could not handle the emotional stress of a personal or family crisis. It may be a divorce, an illness, or a death in the family, but at some point, life will throw you a curve. You will need to make adjustments and transitions in your personal life. Your ability to handle emotional trauma will be a factor in whether or not you can keep your business going during these times.

Always hope for the best, but be prepared for the worst.

In one period of about two years, I lost both of my parents and a brother. At times, it was hard for me to stay focused and keep my business going through all of this adversity, but somehow I made it through. Unfortunately, this is one of those personality traits that you can't really measure until it happens to you.

If you have been through an emotional crisis before, and you were able to find the strength to keep going in the face of adversity, it will be an advantage to your business if and when another such crisis hits. If you tend to become unraveled for an extended period of time during an emotional crisis, it doesn't mean you shouldn't go into business for yourself. But you *should* be aware of your own emotional limitations and how they can affect your business.

THE UNKNOWN

When Christopher Columbus landed in North America, he thought he had discovered India. Still, he is remembered as a very successful explorer. This is what it's like to go into business for yourself. You are continuously setting sail into the Unknown, and many storms lie in your path, but there is also plenty of sunshine. Like the great explorers, you are constantly moving towards unknown shores. Once you have accomplished one goal or objective, you have to turn around and start on a new journey.

Are you someone who enjoys starting new projects and taking on new challenges? Or does it trouble you if you don't know exactly what you will be doing tomorrow, next week, next month, or next year? If you are someone who likes to have everything in a certain routine, who prefers to stick with one job, one employer for as long as you can, then starting a business is probably not for you.

But if you are someone who is comfortable with continuously venturing into the Unknown, starting your own business may be a viable option. It requires certain kinds of courage to be able to venture into uncharted territory time and again. It requires the courage to fail, and also the courage to succeed.

DO YOU FEAR FAILURE?

Are you someone who is afraid of failure? Do you think it's better not to try at all than to risk failing? In your job performance, do you often avoid taking on extra responsibilities, because you're afraid that you might fail? When you are handed a project, do you go all-out to succeed? Or do you just do the bare minimum required to complete the project, because doing any more might put you at risk for failure?

Like competition, failure is one of your best friends. When things are going well, you are not tested. Only when you fail will you find out if you have the resources, perseverance, and mental discipline to bounce back. A self-employed business owner has the *freedom* to fail, but also the free-

Failure is one of your best friends.

dom to try again. One great aspect— but also the most challenging—about running your own business is that you are truly on your own. When you make a mistake, you are the only one who can correct it. *When you fail as the decision-maker, it will be quite apparent where you went wrong. It is then much easier to correct your failure.*

A huge problem with large companies and organizations, especially government organizations, is that too much time is spent *avoiding failure.* People do not want to be blamed for failure, so they spend all their time looking for reasons why something *won't* work, rather than trying something new to see if it *will* work. When I worked as a marketing director for large organizations, very often the marketing and communications plans I developed would be radically changed and altered by managers and executives who were trying to hold onto their jobs. These people were so concerned about *not* failing that they were unwilling to trust me to do the job I had been hired to do.

Once, when I was serving as Public Affairs Director for Metro of Seattle/King County, I was asked to put together a communications plan to inform business owners in downtown Seattle about transportation alternatives Metro was considering to ease downtown traffic congestion. One alternative being considered was a downtown transit-only tunnel that would allow buses to move underneath the city streets. Construction of this tunnel would be the most disruptive option for downtown businesses, but it would also provide the best alternative for easing congestion.

My main goal of the campaign was not to convince downtown business owners that any one alternative was better than the others, but to make sure they were aware of the alternatives being considered and informed of the construction disruption each alternative would cause to their business. To this end, I developed a communications campaign that included direct mail, a monthly newsletter, public notification of our meetings, and one-on-one meetings with downtown business owners. I thought that going door-to-door and visiting with each business owner would be the best way to get our message to the target audience.

When my proposal came back from the board, it had been gutted. The Metro transit officials were only interested in doing the *minimum required by law* to get the transportation alternatives project going. State transportation law required only that we hold a public meeting before starting any type of construction in downtown Seattle. However, we were not required by law to *announce* that meeting to the general public before holding it. I was told, "You can go ahead with the newsletter, but no one-on-one meetings with the business owners, and no notification of the public meeting dates."

The Metro transit officials hoped that by doing only the bare minimum required by law, they could sidestep any conflicts with downtown business owners. They were afraid that the business owners would object to *any* proposed transportation alternative because of the construction disruption it would cause to their businesses. As a result, the Metro officials figured it would be better not to publicize the public meetings. If only a few downtown business owners showed up at these meetings, then fewer objections would be raised to the transportation alternatives project.

I responded that I couldn't be held accountable if downtown business owners showed up at future public meetings complaining they were not informed of the transportation alternatives being considered. If the downtown business owners had thought

Metro was trying to stonewall them, they might band together to fight the project. If they had gone to court for an injunction to stop Metro from starting any downtown construction without their approval, it might have delayed the transportation alternatives project and eventually killed it. And *I* would be the one held responsible for not having properly informed the business owners about the project alternatives.

In the end, I received approval and went ahead with the one-on-one meetings with downtown business owners. Because of those efforts, the business owners were well aware of the transportation alternatives, and no one came to a public meeting complaining they had not been informed of what Metro was planning. When Metro started construction on a transit tunnel under the streets of downtown Seattle, we had the *support* of local businesses. This tunnel has since relieved a great deal of downtown transit congestion by allowing buses to travel underground. I do not want to suggest that I am responsible for the successful construction of the downtown Seattle transit tunnel. That acolade goes to a man by the name of Neil Peterson.

It is far better and much easier to look for ways to do a job right than to spend all your time trying to avoid doing it wrong. As a self-employed business owner, you usually don't have to deal with this level of bureaucracy. You do, however, have to provide your clients and customers with the best product or service possible. And that requires a willingness to take risks. You must offer what you think will be the best solution to your client's needs and take the risk that some part of it will not be quite adequate.

If you do fail in some part of your plan, you will either know how to correct the failure or know how to avoid it the next time around. But *never* be afraid of failure. Failure helps you to identify the ways to improve your product or service. After you've failed, you can use what you've learned from your mistakes to provide a superior product or service in the future. Out of failure comes the means for later success.

DO YOU FEAR SUCCESS?

Are you a person who is afraid of success? Do you boot opportunities away? After you have received a promotion or recognition, are you the type who never quite lives up to expectations?
When you are a self-employed business owner, your ability to
handle success is just as important as your ability to handle
failure or setbacks. Each time you complete a successful project
or assignment, the bar is raised and you subconsciously know
that you will have to perform at an even higher level the next
time around. I know people who have stumbled in business
because they were afraid to keep pushing higher, afraid to perform at higher levels.

I once hired a free agent to help me in selling advertising for
my newspaper. This particular agent worked with me for several years as a sort of "backup" salesperson, providing support
for my own sales efforts. She approached all the potential
advertisers and made all the sales calls I didn't have time to
handle myself. At times, she was a very effective salesperson,
but I started to notice a strange trend. Each time she had an
outstanding month selling advertising for me and was ready to
progress to a higher sales level, she would fall off the edge. I
would call her for a weekly sales meeting, leave a message on
her voice mail, and not hear back from her for several weeks.
And then, just when I was about to give up on her, she would
call me and say that everything was fine.

Usually, by the time she called me back, my newspaper would
be facing its next deadline. All the momentum that she had
gained in selling for the last several issues would be gone, and
she would have to start from scratch. But often, she could still
recover her previous selling pace and make some great sales
under deadline.

On one occasion, I was having a hard time selling advertising
for an upcoming issue of my paper. It seemed that every sales
call I made was either not returned or the potential client was

not interested. Time was running out, and it looked as if this would be the first issue that would not generate a profit. But just before I started production of the paper, I received a call from my salesperson. She had made a number of last-minute sales among her pending clients and had actually outsold me for the first time. This particular issue ended up being the most profitable issue ever.

I couldn't believe it! I told her I was dedicating the issue to her and that I would be stopping by her apartment later that afternoon with a bottle of champagne to celebrate. But when I got to her apartment with the champagne, I discovered that she wasn't home. I called her several times that week and left messages on her voice mail, but once more it was several weeks before I heard from her again. At that point, I decided that I was tired of the roller coaster ride, and we parted company.

People who fear success often like to work under pressure conditions. The problem is that they often *create* these pressure conditions on their own. To succeed in business, you must be able to work under pressure, but chaos should be the exception rather than the rule. The self-employed business owner must have not only the ability but also the *desire* to continually improve themselves. Each time the bar is raised, you must willingly accept the challenge to prove yourself over your last performance. You can't allow yourself to be afraid of success, because eventually, if you work long and hard enough, it *will* come.

CHAPTER TEN

Organization

If the motto for real estate sales is "Location, Location, Location," the motto for starting and maintaining a successful business should be "Organization, Organization, Organization."

Organization, or a lack thereof, often makes the difference between success and failure in business. Success in business is all about developing *systems* that make doing your job and its various tasks easier and more profitable with each passing day. Time *is* money, as they say. And the more organized you are, the faster and easier it will be for you to manage your business and make money.

Organization means opening your daily mail and deciding what to do with it on the spot, instead of letting it stack up a foot high on the desk. It means returning phone calls within twenty-four hours and not letting phone messages back up on your voice mail. It means having a filing system for bills, invoices, receipts, tax records, etc., so you can locate whatever document you need quickly. It means having a Rolodex or file box where you keep the business cards and contact information for all your clients and potential clients. It means having a business card of your own that you can hand out to people—with your company name, address, phone and fax numbers, e-mail address, and web site URL—so they can contact you easily. It means making sure that your car is in working order, so you won't miss important appointments. The more organized you are, the more you can accomplish in a day, a week, or a year.

When you hear that someone is "burned out" from running their own business, it usually means that the business owner is exhausted from the daily effort of trying to run a disorganized business. A business owner who is disorganized is continuously flailing away like the worst government bureaucrats or people who work for large organizations. These people can afford to be disorganized because their salary is not based on organizational ability. For the self-employed business owner, organizational ability is an essential survival tool. I firmly believe that being organized is one of the major reasons I am still in business today.

> **I firmly believe that being organized is one of the major reasons I am still in business today.**

Being organized also instills a sense of confidence in your clients and potential clients, while not being organized tends to have the opposite effect. There is a print shop across the street from my office. Each time I visit this print shop, I see empty and unplugged computers, diskettes stacked everywhere, and papers and files spread out across the desks and piled on the floor behind the counters. The entire shop has a look of general chaos. I no longer use this print shop for large projects where I have to leave an original set of documents with them. I'm afraid that they will misplace or lose my documents. I often wonder how many other customers they have lost because of their poor organizational skills.

Riding in someone else's vehicle tells me a lot about whether or not I want to work with them on a professional basis. If the car is relatively clean on the outside, and if the inside is not littered with fast-food wrappers and old newspapers, it tells me that this person is organized and pays attention to detail. If someone is organized enough to make sure that their car is presentable, I imagine that their home and office are probably also organized as well. If I conduct business with this person, my project with them will probably be completed in an orderly manner.

THE INDUSTRIAL REVOLUTION IS OVER

When you own your own business, you often feel like you are on the outside of the business world looking in. You start to see how outdated much of the routine of conducting business really is. Most businesses still run on the Industrial Revolution and assembly-line models. Assembly lines require that all employees show up at the exact same time, for obvious reasons. One employee's absence can shut down a whole operation. For some reason, we seem to think that this model should apply to office workers as well.

In the past twenty years, technology has advanced to the point where most of us could work from our homes if we wanted to. With the right software and the security codes needed to access our company's computer network, most of us would have no trouble telecommuting every day. Yet we still feel obliged to get into our single-occupancy vehicles and fight our way through traffic every morning to spend all day in an office cubicle. In most companies, employees are still required to be at their desks by 8 AM and usually go home around 5 PM, just the way it was a hundred years ago. This is a huge waste of time. Using your time wisely is not only a precious resource; it is also a major competitive advantage.

IT'S ALL ABOUT TIME

Organization is about having perhaps not a strict schedule, but a good idea of how you use your time each day. Time is your most precious commodity, and wasting time is a business killer. This doesn't mean, however, that you have to work fifteen-hour days, seven days a week. I am working fewer hours today than at any time in the history of my business, but I am making the most of my time. Therefore, I am also making more money than I have ever made.

Time management is as basic as thinking through your commute to your workplace. If you work in a large urban area, the curse of the long commute is probably the biggest time waster of all.

I generally get up around 5:30 to 6 AM and work in my home office until 8 AM. I find that I am at my best intellectually during this time, that I am more alert earlier in the day. On most mornings, I complete over two hours of work before most people even arrive at their offices. There are few interruptions like phone calls this early in the morning, and I actually get more accomplished during this time than at any other time of the day. (I've written a good part of this book during my early-morning work period.)

At 8:45 AM, my commute to downtown Seattle is less than ten minutes. By this time, most people are at work, and traffic has thinned out to the point that I don't have to wait around in traffic jams. If I were to take the same route at an earlier time, say around 7 AM, my commute could last up to an hour. Likewise, for my evening commute, I usually go home around 6 PM, so I don't have to deal with evening traffic.

The time of your daily commute may not seem important, but again it's the small things that add up. Time management decisions like this *can* make the difference between success and failure. Let's say that, by taking a later commute, I save myself two hours per day that I would normally spend stuck in traffic. Two hours times five days per week times fifty weeks per year = 500 hours per year. In one year, I have saved time equivalent to over twenty-one days. In about twelve years[1], I will have saved almost one full year in productive time, just by timing my daily

---

[1] Calculations based on working 260 days per year. (5 days per week X 50 weeks per year)

commute so that I don't have to travel during peak traffic periods. This doesn't even factor in the extra time and efficiency that I gain by working without interruptions between 6 and 8 AM.

I very seldom have downtime unless I want it. On the rare occasion that I do get stuck in traffic, I still try to use that time productively. I turn on the radio, listen to radio ads, and compare them to the ones I've produced. Perhaps I can borrow a pointer or two from the ads I hear. If I'm stuck in a long line at the grocery store, I try use that time productively as well. For example, I might start thinking about my book and how I can express my thoughts and ideas more clearly in the chapter I'm working on. This usually works until I start mumbling to myself, at which point the people who have been waiting in line with me suddenly start to migrate to other lines.

PAY YOUR BILLS

Get into the habit of paying your bills on time. Sometimes this is easier said than done, but it is a habit that you should develop early on, especially when you own your own business. If you do fall behind in your bills, prioritize your payments and communicate with the financial institutions or parties to whom you owe money. You will minimize the damage if you keep in touch with your billers and make them aware of your financial situation. After all, if you can't meet your obligations, *you* are the one who has failed to live up to your end of the agreement. Don't put the people that you owe money to in the position of guessing when and if they are going to be paid.

You can always pay *some* amount of money towards a debt, even if it is only a small amount. People can be very be understanding and supportive if you communicate with them and make them aware of your circumstances. They tend to be just the opposite if you keep them in the dark.

Always be accountable for your actions. If ultimately your business fails and you have to close down for whatever reason,

HONOR YOUR OBLIGATIONS. If you go back to work for a regular full-time employer, work out a payment plan with the parties you still owe. Pay them back, even if it takes fifty years. There are few things worse in this world than individuals who don't pay their debts. These people often leave others short of the money they need to pay THEIR debts, creating a vicious chain of unpaid debts that eventually affects us all.

> **There are few things worse in this world than individuals who don't pay their debts. These people often leave others short of the money they need to pay THEIR debts, creating a vicious chain of unpaid debts that eventually affects us all.**

If your business fails, but you still honor your obligations and pay off your debts, your path will be much easier if you decide to start another business in the future. People forgive, but they don't forget. If you make good on your financial commitments, people will *trust* you. Once that trust is broken, you can never get it back.

If you get into the routine of really feeling the pain when you make a financial mistake, it is unlikely that you will make the same mistake again. If you write off a debt, or take the easy way out by declaring bankruptcy, or by changing the name of your company as some lawyers will advise you to do in order to skirt your obligations, you are likely to repeat that mistake numerous times. It's all a mindset of how much responsibility you are willing to take for your actions when things go wrong.

I recently received a call from a good friend of mine who had just become the executive director of a non-profit organization. His first words to me were: "I should have listened to you." Since we hadn't talked in several months, I didn't know what he was talking about. He said that his non-profit organization had held a series of large fundraising events and had lost close to $90,000. He reminded me of our conversation several months before these events.

Since I had previous experience as a director of a non-profit organization, he had asked me for some advice on programming and fundraising. I had told him, since he was just starting out as director of the non-profit, that he should take *small, incremental steps* and keep his fundraising efforts very simple. I suggested that he should not spread the organization or himself too thin. I remember suggesting that it would be better for his non-profit to conduct one, or maybe two events in the first year. If these events proved successful, he could expand to more events in the following years.

When he called back several months later, my friend told me that he ended up doing the exact opposite of what I had advised. He had planned several fundraisers within the first few months of taking over the non-profit. For these events, he had brought in a number of out-of-town bands and entertainers. But attendance to the events had been poor, and the amount of money raised at these fundraisers was not enough to cover the cost of putting them on. His non-profit ended up losing a considerable amount of money, and what was worse, he still owed money to the bands, entertainers, and other people who had helped with the events.

He then asked me what he should he do now. I told him to develop a plan to pay off every artist, vendor, newspaper, or anyone else he owes money to. He must pay off his debts for this year before he even thinks about next year's events. Only by paying off the people he owes can he hope to re-establish his reputation as an effective and accountable manager. Once he has paid off his debts, he will be in a position to start over and to rebuild his non-profit slowly and steadily, having learned from his mistakes.

One final word of caution about paying your bills on time. Don't fall behind on your obligations to the bank or any other financial institution. It takes many years to develop good credit, but if you make just a few late payments, your good standing is history. It's completely unfair, but that's the way it is.

MEETINGS

Meetings are sometimes necessary, but they can be a huge time-waster. Certainly, it is essential for your clients to see you in the flesh now and then. And there are times when you *must* meet with your clients to plan a project, get consensus and feedback on ideas, etc. But as a self-employed business owner, you must be careful. You can't afford to waste time sitting in meetings that do nothing to increase the profitability of your business. Again, you must guard your time like a pit bull; don't let other people waste it.

Meetings are the second-biggest time-wasters in business, next to sitting in traffic. Some business people are professional meeting-goers. They spend over 70 percent of their time in meetings. A lot of money is wasted in meetings as well. For example, if ten people with an average hourly wage of $85 per hour attend a two-hour meeting, it costs the company $1,700.

When someone calls you for a meeting or coffee, ask yourself, "Do I *really* need to meet with this person? Or can we accomplish what we need to do by talking over the phone?" I realize that some business owners (e.g., sales consultants) may need to take more meetings than others. But you must learn to weed out the meetings that are not crucial to fulfilling your clients' needs and making your business grow.

SEMINARS MAKE OTHER PEOPLE RICH

Seminars are another example of a time-waster that takes you away from your business. Many times seminars are held in distant cities, requiring you to pay for a hotel, meals, and travel in order to attend them. Even those seminars that are held in your area are often expensive. The concept of a seminar is enticing.

You can learn new skills while meeting people in your industry and networking with the best!

While seminars are certainly more honest than those get-rich-quick schemes that you see on TV infomercials, the end result is the same. Seminars are designed to make money for the people who host them. Very often, the lessons taught at seminars are things that you should already know or could learn by yourself with a minimum of effort. For instance, rather than spending $750 plus travel expenses for a sales seminar, you could just as easily learn sales techniques by buying $50 worth of good sales instruction books at your local bookstore or reading a good, college-level sales textbook.

Before you attend a seminar, take a close look at what is being offered. Unless a seminar offers to teach you things that you know you can't learn on your own, it is better to save your time and money.

CEO = CHIEF OF SALES

Your most important role as CEO of your company is as the Chief of Sales. Your primary function will always be to sell your product or service. No one else can possibly represent your business the way you yourself can, so don't abdicate that responsibility to someone else. If you don't like selling or schmoozing, stick with your current job.

No matter how high-tech we become, sales is still about developing and nurturing relationships with your clients and potential clients. People buy from other people, not from machines. Being the Chief of Sales is the most challenging aspect of any business. Typically, corporate salespeople are well paid because they deserve it. If you can't get people to pay for your product or service, your business will amount to nothing.

The best salespeople view themselves as consultants rather than salespeople. This is an important mindset. Obviously, your products or services are of value, or you wouldn't be offering them. Correct? If this is true, then you are not really trying to sell anything, but to make your target audience aware of your products or services. It is up to them to decide if your products or services will benefit them. It may be that what you offer has little value to a potential client at this particular moment, but may be of use to them in the future. Don't give up! Keep checking back with your potential client every few months or so. Circumstances change.

If you can't get people to pay for your product or service, your business will amount to nothing.

I once had a potential client that I absolutely *knew* would benefit from advertising in my newspaper, and later on my radio show. I never harassed them, but I would check in with them every six months or so, to see if they were ready to come on board. Finally, after *eight years*, the client had a new directive from the home office to achieve more local exposure. My radio show became a perfect vehicle for them.

As Chief of Sales, your goal should be to position yourself as the expert in your field. No one should even consider going to someone else. In my case, I promote Casey Communications as the leading expert in radio. No agency in the United States can create, secure, and execute radio programming better than Casey Communications.

Often, it is what you do *after* your first meeting with a potential client, or *after* you've made a sale, that will determine how the client sees you and whether or not they will do further business with you. For example, if you are a real estate broker, you would do well to keep in touch with people who have bought houses or property from you, or even anyone who has expressed interest in doing so.

Buying a home is probably the largest investment that anyone will ever make in their lifetime. But when it comes to selling homes, many real estate brokers have the sales mentality of a door-to-door vacuum salesman. Once the transaction is completed, the client never hears from their realtor again. In fact, this is where the relationship should just be beginning. The average family in the United States moves every five to seven years. Most family moves are made within the same community.

Therefore, if you are a real estate broker, you will have an edge over your competition if you think of the home buyer as a client rather than a customer. You should position yourself as the expert consultant in all matters of residential real estate. If a client wants to know how much their home has appreciated, they should call you first. If they are moving to Santa Barbara, California, and have a question about real estate there, they should call you about it.

A quarterly newsletter would be of great value here, to keep your existing and possible future clients up-to-date on topics of interest to home owners. For example, in the spring issue, you could include an article about the best shrubbery to plant for the summer after an unseasonably cold and wet winter. In the fall issue, you could have updates on interest rates for the third quarter. You might include a report on legislation in the state capital that would reduce property taxes for your clients. Perhaps you could publish the number of home sales in a particular neighborhood. Each edition of your newsletter could include a question-and-answer column and a profile of a family that just bought a house through your brokerage. The more you establish yourself as being *the* expert to consult when it comes to real estate, the more your clients will return to you for help in their home-buying needs.

YOU DON'T NEED ME

As Chief of Sales, it is also important to tell a potential client when your product or service is *not* a good fit for them. In my profession, this means telling a very small businessman that radio advertising would not be their best or most cost-effective marketing option. When I see someone who hasn't really thought about what they want to accomplish with their business, I decline to become their business consultant.

Again, it's good business to be honest. Word gets around and people trust you. When people trust you, good things happen. When people *don't* trust you, the opposite also happens. Bad news spreads much faster than good news. If a client has a bad experience with your services, it's very hard to control the damage.

SALES TACTICS

One way in which my business has changed for me in the past five years is that I am currently in the position of being *sold to*, rather than selling. Account executives from across the country now try to sell me on the virtues of their radio stations for some of my larger clients. I have learned some very important lessons from radio salespeople that will help me when the day comes that I return to the selling mode.

For example, I've discovered that I have good instincts when it comes to selling. I respect other people's time. When I call someone, I always ask if this is a good time to talk with them, rather than just launching into my sales pitch, as many salespeople do. If a potential client tells me that they would like to learn more about my company, I am brief and to the point. I make a quick summary of my services, and then refer them to my web site at caseycommunications.net, where they can find out more information about my company at their convenience.

In talking to other salespeople, I have also learned about areas for improvement in my own sales techniques. For instance, I have occasionally received a phone call from a radio salesperson when I was in the midst of a deadline. I wanted to learn more about their station, but I was too busy to return their call as quickly as I should have. When they called me back, I was grateful for their persistence. Looking back on selling advertising for my newspaper and my radio program, I remember times where, if a person didn't return my phone call, I assumed they weren't interested. I now realize that in some cases, I should have pressed more. When I return to selling, I will be more persistent.

This leads to another subtle nuance of selling. Very few times will someone reject you outright. They reject you by not returning your follow-up calls. Only after you call them four or five times and they don't call back do you start to get the hint. One thing I've learned is that most people would prefer to have their businesses run on auto-pilot. If you are presenting a new idea, the biggest resistance usually comes from having to make the client think about something new. Here they had everything in their business neatly set up for the week, the month, or the year, and suddenly you come along and upset the apple cart with a new idea for them to consider.

I understand this way of thinking better today—because now *I* am the lazy one. Sometimes when I am in the midst of a radio ad campaign, I get a call from a radio salesperson who tells me that their station would be the perfect broadcast venue for my client's commercials. Usually, by the time they call me, the budget for the ad campaign has been set, or the broadcast stations for the commercials have been selected, and I am reluctant to do extra work to include this new station in the campaign plan. Not only do I have to make the adjustments with my vendors, I have to go back to the client for their approval of the changes. I am always concerned that when I do this, the client may respond by saying, "Why didn't you think of using this new radio station in the first place?"

However, I will seriously consider the salesperson's proposal if they can convince me that their station will bring some "added value" to the radio campaign. It helps if the salesperson is well-prepared. I will certainly listen to them if they have done some background research on the client, and if they understand what we are trying to accomplish with this particular ad campaign.

It also helps if the salesperson keeps their pitch clear and concise. If they send me a one-page summary of their station (as opposed to a fifteen-page fax), I will certainly look it over. Perhaps their regular listeners are among the target audience that my client is trying to reach, or the station has a genuine interest in the campaign message. If they can break down my resistance and show me the benefits of advertising with their station, I will be more than willing to do the extra work to include them in the campaign.

THE BEST TIMES TO MAKE SALES CALLS

The best time to make sales calls is between 9:15 and 11:30 AM on weekdays. Before 9:15 AM, potential clients are usually getting organized for the day. They spend this time in meetings or chatting with co-workers or just "zoning out" in front of their computers. After 11:30 AM, they are either on their way to lunch or thinking very heavily about it.

The second best time to make sales calls is between 1:30 and 3:30 PM. After 3:30 PM, most people are making a mental shift towards going home for the evening. Also, avoid calling people on Monday mornings and on Friday afternoons.

As you can see, there is actually a very small window of opportunity to make the most effective sales calls. This is another reason why it is important to be organized and to use your time wisely. You must plan your work schedule to be able to reach clients at the time of day when they will be the most willing to listen to you.

FIND THE CHIEF

Whenever possible, you should go straight to the decision-maker when trying to make a sale. This is sometimes difficult. Often, the person with the title "Marketing Director" or "Sales Director" is a gatekeeper. They have been assigned to keep salespeople from bothering the higher-level executives. It is their *job* to say no. It can be tricky to try to find the right person to talk to, because you don't want to appear to be going over someone's head.

You must sometimes get creative when trying to reach the decision-makers. When I was publishing my newspaper, I had a very effective strategy for getting in touch with potential advertisers. I would call up the CEO of the company and ask to interview them for the paper. Since the company was usually targeting the same audience as my newspaper, the CEO would often have valuable information that would be of interest to my readers.

Even if the CEO of the company had never heard of my publication, they would usually agree to the interview. After the interview was over, they would often ask questions about my publication and its history. On many occasions, the CEO would then suggest that I meet with their marketing director, so they could consider advertising in my newspaper. (You are on the right track when an executive asks one of their subordinates to take a look at your company or your proposal.)

When I called the marketing director to make an appointment, my first words were to say that their CEO had asked me call. I always got the appointment, and usually the sale as well.

LISTENING TO YOUR CLIENT

To succeed in business, you must be a good listener. When I first started my business, I confess that I did not have good listening skills. I would meet with potential clients and quickly launch into my sales pitch about how they could benefit from advertising in my newspaper. While I never tried to oversell my publication, I did not spend enough time listening to the clients and finding out their wants and needs. I think this may have hurt me at times. A client is less likely to do business with you if they sense that you are only interested in pitching your product or service to them. You must look for the ways that your product or service can benefit *their* specific business.

Over the years, I have become a better listener. Now, when I meet with a potential client, I ask them to tell me everything they can about their company before I start into my sales pitch. Once I know the details of their business, it becomes easier for me to talk about the different ways that radio advertising can benefit their company.

I can always tell when a salesperson is *not* listening to me. For example, I call up a car dealership to ask about buying a used car, and before I have even started to describe what I am looking for, the salesperson says, "That's great! You know, I've got a 1994 Chevrolet Camaro down here that would be just perfect for you. It's only got 30,000 miles on it, and it runs like a dream. But you've got to get down here within the next hour to see it. It'll be gone by tomorrow."

Or, I'll be dealing with a real estate broker, trying to buy a new house. I tell them that I really need a house in West Seattle to preserve the short commute time to my office. A few days later, I get a call from the real estate broker. "I've got a terrific house up in North Seattle that you really *must* see!" As you can probably guess, my dealings with salespeople who don't listen to their clients tend to be very short.

The ability to listen to your clients is especially important in those all-too-frequent occasions when your client can't quite articulate what they want or need for a certain project. Often, you must ask questions to get your client to think about the dynamics of a project and what they really hope to accomplish with it. The questions you ask will depend on the type of business you own. In my case, planning a radio ad campaign for a client means asking them who their target audience is, what the features of their product or service are, etc.

Before you begin the actual work on a project, you must make sure both you and your client understand the end goal and you both agree on what will be done to meet that end goal. If you and your client have different ideas about what you will accomplish, it can lead to trouble. Hair-styling is a good example of this. Often, hairstylists project what *they* like in a particular hairstyle, but they sometimes fail to listen to their clients. And of course, the client sometimes has trouble articulating exactly what they want done to their hair.

If the client is not happy with the end result of their hairstyle, it is often because the stylist did not listen to the client's requests. The best hairstylists are those that go out of their way to establish a dialogue with their clients and to make sure that the client understands what will be done to their hair *before* it is done. This is especially important when the client wants to make a dramatic change in their hairstyle. If the client feels that the stylist did not listen to them before doing the job, the client will not come back to that hairstylist again.

SELL WHAT PEOPLE NEED

A friend of mine who thought he knew me well used to say, "Casey, you could sell ice cubes to Eskimos." While he may have thought that he was complimenting me on my persuasive and leadership skills, I took it as an insult. He seemed to suggest that I could con people into buying things that they didn't need.

I never want to sell anything to anyone who doesn't need my services. It takes too much effort to sell people things that they really don't need. Like a thief, you just have to work too hard. This is why many good people shy away from sales. The words "salesperson" garners images of the door-to-door salespeople who try to sell you a vacuum cleaner or magazine subscriptions that you don't really need, or of the pesky telemarketers who call during dinner to try to sell us a new long-distance plan. People are afraid that, even if they try to sell their potential clients or customers products or services that they *do* need, they will be seen in the same bad light as salespeople who try to sell people what they *don't* need.

I used to frequent a particular resort in Mexico, where the local beach hawkers were constantly trying to sell the tourists an endless stream of items. After a while, I noticed that each of these salespeople was selling a slightly different version of the same items: Carpets, t-shirts, jewelry, and souvenir trinkets. Nowhere did I see anyone selling items that people on the beach might *really* need. It occurred to me that a salesperson at this resort might have done very well selling bottles of suntan oil, sunglasses, soft drinks, bottled water, beach towels, sandals, or baseball caps.

This should be your strategy as well. Think through what your potential clients *really* need, and try to find a need that is not being met. The more creative you are at identifying a legitimate need and filling it, the more successful your business will be.

TECHNOLOGY: THE GOOD, THE BAD, AND THE UGLY

In the past twenty years, nothing has allowed more businesses to succeed—or to fail—than advancements in technology. The technology explosion of the past two decades has made it possible for more people to start their own businesses than ever before. There is no way, practically or financially, that I ever could have published a newspaper if it were not for the incredible leaps made in desktop publishing and other technologies around the time I started my business.

Affordable computers, pagers, and cell phones have allowed people to become instantly accessible to anyone. With home office equipment and voice mail, we no longer have to pay for a receptionist or an answering service to organize our business, schedule appointments, and take calls as we did in the old days. Thanks to technology, we can now conduct our business anytime, anywhere.

But like anything else, too much of a good thing can be a curse. There is a difference between technology use and technology abuse. I have seen people fail in business because they didn't know how to use technology properly. No matter how far it advances, technology is still only a tool for delivering products or services. *Technology starts to fail us when the technology itself becomes the master of the business, and the product or service becomes secondary.*

Before you purchase any type of technology for your business, ask yourself, "Will this technology really make my business run more smoothly? Or will it actually make things more complicated?" Do you *really* need a cell phone that can access the Internet and send e-mails? Or will this techno-toy distract you from making sales calls and getting projects completed for your clients? Should you really use an accounting program like Quickbooks to keep track of your income and expenses? Or would it be more cost-effective to find a bookkeeper or an accountant to watch over your money? Be very discriminating with technology. In many cases, technology is a distraction and often responsible for entrepreneurs doing a lot of unnecessary and unproductive work.

A PUBLISHER'S STORY

About the time I started my newspaper, there was a publisher in the office next door to me who started publishing his own bimonthly newspaper. When I first started my publication, I would input the entire copy for each issue of my paper into my laptop. My fellow publisher did the same with his publication. After a few issues, I realized that I was spending way too much time inputting articles into the computer and not enough time making sales calls to sell advertising for my paper.

Given the choice, I would have preferred to just sit at my desk all day and input articles into my laptop. It was easy and repetitive, and very relaxing. On the other hand, selling was hard, and cold-calling was particularly challenging for me. I had to remind myself that my newspaper was a *business*, not a hobby. As CEO of the company, I was responsible for making sales calls if my newspaper was going to survive.

I hired a free agent to do the inputting job for me at $25 per hour. It cost me about $200 per issue, but it saved me twenty to twenty-five hours per issue in computer time. I also paid a proofreader $50 per issue to catch typos and grammatical errors. This freed up the time I needed to make sales calls, visit with potential clients, and sell advertising. Meanwhile, my fellow publisher was happy to just sit behind his computer all day, inputting his newspaper and waiting for the phone to ring with possible advertisers. But the phone didn't ring, and very shortly, his newspaper went out of business.

As a business owner, you can't allow yourself to be seduced by technology. If you find, as I did, that your business has a number of repetitive tasks that take you away from your essential duties as CEO of your company, it would be best to hire a free agent to handle them for you. (A good rule of thumb is to hire a free agent to execute *any* tasks that are repetitive.) Your first priority is to *manage your business and keep it going.* Technology may be time-saving, cost-effective, and occasionally fun to dabble with. But always remember, it is only a means to an end, not the end itself.

READY, AIM, SEND!

Another downside of technology is the explosion in e-mails. Every day, we can receive hundreds of e-mails, mostly from people we don't know. The worst of it, of course, is known as "spam" (named after a Monty Python song in which the word "Spam," referring to the infamous pressed ham product, is repeated over and over). Most spam e-mail messages contain advertisements for products, services, or web sites that nobody in their right mind would even *think about* using or looking at in a million years. Most of us simply delete spam from our Inbox without even looking at the attached message.

But spam aside, e-mail is like any other technology tool. It can make conducting our business easier, but it can also hurt us if we don't use it correctly. I know a number of people who use e-mail as a substitute for doing their job. They spend their days sending out e-mails and responding to messages from friends and business associates. They measure their job performance by the number of e-mails they send or respond to. It makes them feel important, when in fact they are just wasting time. If you wish to be a successful business owner, you can't spend four hours a day on your e-mail.

One of the most effective uses for e-mail is as a means to send your potential clients a summary of your products or services. You can attach a résumé and samples of your work, and even include a link to your web site in the e-mail message. But e-mail should never be used as a *substitute* for regular sales tactics. You must still make cold calls, go to chamber of commerce meetings, visit with clients, and check back with them every few months in order to sell your business.

Never send an e-mail describing your products or services to someone unless you have called or met with them first to introduce yourself. If you send a "cold e-mail" to a potential client, it will probably be deleted with all the other Spam that they receive on a daily basis. After you have contacted a client and sent an e-mail to them, you should always call them back a few days later, to verify that they received the e-mail. And never assume just because you've sent them an e-mail with your contact info that a client will automatically think of *you* when they have a need for your type of product or service.

Also, I strongly urge you to resist the temptation to send e-mail jokes, sports scores, political views, or inspirational messages to your current or potential clients. If you are continually sending out non-related business e-mails, you are screaming to your clients that you have a lot of extra time on your hands. If you are currently working on a project with a certain client, they may start to wonder why you aren't working on their account with all this extra time. Even if you're not working on a project with that client, you are still wasting their time by forcing them to skim and delete your e-mails.

PHONE ETIQUETTE & VOICE MESSAGING

I am against the death penalty, with one exception: I would openly advocate public executions for all violators of phone etiquette.

As a self-employed business owner, you must remember to treat every potential business contact as if they are the most important person on the planet, especially when you are talking to them on the phone. Businesses and organizations change at a rapid pace. You don't want to alienate people with bad phone manners. The person you put on hold today might be a future executive or even a CEO.

Here are some tips for good phone etiquette. (Follow these tips and, if my "death penalty" wish ever becomes law, you'll never end up in front of the firing squad.)

- If you are on the phone with someone, *NEVER* put them on hold to take another call unless you are in a life-or-death situation. Let your voice-mail take the message and return the other call *after* you have completed your current conversation.

- *NEVER* bring a cell phone to a meeting with a client and take calls during the meeting. Your client will count it as a point against doing business with you. (There are people who have done this to me. They are absolutely clueless that this is the major reason I will not work with them or send them any business.)

- Also, *NEVER* take calls on your cell phone during lunch. You will annoy not only the person you are having lunch with, but also the people around you in the restaurant. Whenever I see someone taking calls on their cell phone during lunch or dinner, I have to resist a sudden urge to grab their phone and toss it into the soup tureen!

- Use Call Forwarding to forward your office number to your cell phone or home number. This makes it easier for the client to contact you, and they only have to remember one phone number. In fifteen years, I've used one single phone number for my business.

- Use voice-mail instead of an answering machine. Voice-mail only costs about $7 a month. It never misses a call, you never have to change batteries, and it never cuts a caller off before they finish their message.

- Make your voice-mail message quick and to the point. Don't give callers your daily itinerary. Which of the following voice-mail messages would you rather listen to? (The first, by the way, is an actual voice-mail message. The name has been changed to protect the guilty.)

"Hi, this is Steve. I will be out of the office for most of the day attending meetings all morning and afternoon, but I will back in the office all day tomorrow. After a 9 AM staff meeting, I will be available for most of the day and will be checking in for messages. If you need to get in touch with me immediately, my cell phone number is 304-678-4567, or you can reach me by paging me. My pager number is 304-557-9876, extension 234993. My e-mail address is steve@meetings.com. Please leave your name, phone number, and time that you called and I will get back to you as soon as possible. Have a good one."

OR

"Hi, this is Paul Casey, please leave a message."

On the subject of voice-mail, if you go out of town on business or vacation, don't feel compelled to let the whole world know about it. Again, when I go out of town, I still check my e-mails and phone messages at least twice a day. Technology has made it possible for me to conduct business effectively no matter where I am.

Here's another odd voice-mail message that I recently came across:

"Hi, this is Fred. I will be out on vacation the week of April 1st. Please leave your name and number and I will return your call when I return."

This wouldn't have been so bad—except that I called on May 25th!

CHAPTER ELEVEN

The Pitfalls of Partnerships

Real entrepreneurs don't need partners. Partnerships *destroy* businesses and are counterproductive to sustaining your business. It is human nature to want a friend or confidant to go down the unknown path with you, but resist this temptation at all costs. If you feel that you *absolutely must have* a partner to succeed, you probably don't have the necessary confidence or independence it takes to be successful in business anyway.

Many people feel obligated to take on a partner because they feel that the partner will bring camaraderie or some knowledge or skill to the business that they don't have. But often, this "essential knowledge or skill" can be found elsewhere. For instance, you might feel it is necessary to bring in a partner with strong accounting skills because you yourself have no background in accounting. But it would be easier and less expensive in the long run to find a free agent accountant or bookkeeper instead.

The problem with partnerships is that you are essentially giving away half your business before you start. Generally, under a partnership agreement, your partner receives half of all income for your business. If you earn $2000 on a project, your partner receives $1000 of that, whether the partner did any work on the project or not. Of course, the reverse may be true. You could be receiving half the money that your partner earned on an assignment for which you did nothing. But it would be much better for you to keep the $2000 (minus expenses) that *you* have earned, instead of instantly giving half of it away.

If you and your partner are working together on assignments, you are invariably providing your clients with two workers for the price of one. For example, say you own a marketing consulting firm, and a local software company pays you $5000 to develop a marketing plan. You and your partner do equal work on the project and split the $5000. However, as a marketing specialist, you could have just as easily created a marketing plan *all by yourself* and earned the same $5000 as a sole business owner. If you are an expert at what you do—if you have the competence to deliver a good product or service and enough experience in your field to be able to start your own business—you don't *need* to share your job duties or your profits with a partner.

Having a partner means that you create a lot of unnecessary expenses for your business. Everything that you needed before must now be *doubled.* You now need *two* computers, *two* desks, *two* office chairs, *two* phone lines. Whereas before you might have needed to rent an office suite with a single office, now you will need a double-office suite—at double the rent! This kind of high overhead can kill your business very quickly.

Let's take a look at a hypothetical example of this. The following might be a typical monthly budget for a marketing specialist who is a sole business owner. Again, the marketing specialist has just earned $5000 for developing a marketing campaign for a software company.

Office rent	$750
Utilities	$150
Phone	$100
Computer payment	$200
Computer software	$200

Office supplies	$150
Internet expenses	$20
Payments to free agents	$1000
TOTAL	$2570

TOTAL PROFIT FROM $5000 INCOME: $2430

Now here's a monthly budget for a partnership, with the same kinds of expenses and the same amount of income. Again, most of the expenses must now be doubled because there are two business owners instead of one.

Office rent (double office)	$1500
Utilities	$300
Phone	$200
Computer payments	$400
Computer software	$400
Office supplies	$300
Internet expenses	$40
Payments to free agents	$1000
TOTAL	$4140

TOTAL PROFIT FROM $5000 INCOME: $860

AMOUNT EACH PARTNER RECEIVES: $430.

You see the problem? With partnerships, the double expenses cut severely into your business. Each partner receives only a fraction of the profit that either of them would receive as a sole proprietor. This combination of high expenses and low profits makes it extremely difficult for a business to survive in the long term.

Aside from the financial obligations, a partnership can bring other problems. First, a partner adds another layer to the decision making process. You will *always* need your partner's approval before taking on any new clients, investing in new technologies, subscribing to new services, etc. Inevitably, there will be clashes between partners over which clients to deal with, whom to hire and fire, how to provide the best product or service to your clients, and so on. It is much better for the business if *one* person is in charge and has the power to make the decisions.

As I've said before, businesses change over time. The business you start today will be much different from the business you will have five years from now. It will change and grow and move in many different directions. Even if you and your partner have the same vision and goals for your business today, your separate visions and goals will inevitably change as the years go by. Before long, the odds are that you will want to move your business in one direction, while your partner will want to move the business in another direction. I have seen most partnerships work for only short periods of time. Invariably, they break apart when the partners can't agree on the best way to further develop and continue their business together.

If the business survives the breakup, one of the partners usually inherits the business. The partner who takes over the company is now in the same position that they would have been if they had started the business *without* a partner in the first place. The only difference is, now they may have to buy the other partner out. The expense of buying out one-half of a partnership increases your overhead and only makes it more difficult to make money in the future.

Even if a partnership defies the odds and lasts longer than usual, something will inevitably happen to break up the business. If a partner dies (as sometimes happens), very often their half of the partnership will be acquired by the partner's spouse or children. More than likely, the partner has drawn up a will declaring that their spouse or children will inherit their assets, including the business. Your partner's wife, husband, or children may actually end up being your business partner. There are numerous horror stories of businesses that have been destroyed when one partner's family members inherit the partner's half of the business. Those family members end up ruining the business because they are only interested in its assets and have no interest in running the business itself.

Having a partner brings too many negative elements to your business, elements that can severely inhibit your success. It is best to avoid these elements and go it alone. As a sole business owner, you alone will be responsible for the success or failure of your business. Again this may seem scary at times, but it is actually an advantage. With a partnership, you must work twice as hard to make your business successful, and you must overcome twice the disadvantages. Your business will always be dependent on your partner's success as well as your own. As a sole business owner, you at least have the freedom to try, to fail, and to try again *without* encountering the disadvantages that come from having a partner.

> **Having a partner brings too many negative elements to your business, elements that can severely inhibit your success.**

FAMILY & FRIENDS ARE FOR THANKSGIVING

Another pitfall to avoid is including friends and family in the *day-to-day* operations of your business. Your parents, brothers, and sisters can be your best allies, but also your worst critics. While they may outwardly support what you are doing, often they think you are slightly crazy to be starting your own business and wonder when you will go back to a "real job." When they give you advice, they might think that they are doing what is best for you, but their comments can be very harmful. "Well, you know, you never were very good at this or that." "I don't really think you can make a living doing what you're doing." "You never could balance a checkbook."

Families and friends are for Thanksgiving and Christmas. Never go into business with a family member or a friend. Just because you have a personal or family relationship with someone does *not* mean that they will make a good business partner or that they will necessarily have sound business advice for you. I am very grateful to my own family because they have always been hands-off in the day-to-day operations of my business. If you want advice about your business, talk to a small business consultant or to someone who runs a small business with a product or service similar to yours.

BOARD OF DIRECTORS /ADVISORS

Another business killer is appointing a board of directors or advisors with formal or informal oversight responsibilities of your business operations. I have read business books about starting your own business that suggest that you should appoint a board of directors to meet monthly or quarterly to provide you with counsel and advice for your business. I couldn't disagree more.

As a self-employed business owner, you probably don't need to worry about appointing a board of directors, even if your business is successful enough that it seems as if you should turn it into a corporation. Boards are for large corporations and non-profits that can afford the slow decision-making process. Boards often spend all their time telling you what you should *not* do, rather than what you *should* do. They prevent you from making decisions and also from making mistakes. As I've said before, it's better to try new things and learn from your mistakes than it is to spend all your time trying to *avoid* mistakes and thus accomplishing nothing.

When you own your own business, *you* are the decision-maker. This is a huge responsibility, but it is also a competitive advantage in that you can get things done faster and with less trouble than you would in a large corporation. It may be difficult for you to suddenly find yourself in the role of sole decision-maker, especially if you have just left a corporate or government job where a large staff or board of directors made all the important decisions. But the sooner you get into the habit of being a decision-maker on your own, the better off you will be.

While you shouldn't bother with a board of directors, it may help you to occasionally think of yourself as a "Chairperson of the Board" and to ask yourself the kinds of questions that a board of directors would ask. (e.g., "Where do we want our business to be in six months? What goals would we like to accomplish in the next year that we haven't been able to accomplish within the last year?")

It may sound strange, but I sometimes hold "board meetings," featuring only myself, to answer questions like these and to plan strategies for the growth of my business. I sit alone in my office and ask myself questions as if I were addressing an invisible board of directors. In this way, I am able to clarify my thoughts about various problems and to examine my options for solving them. (I usually keep the office door closed during these "board meetings," so that people in the neighboring offices will not look in and wonder if they should call the men in the white coats.)

As a business owner, you should also resist the temptation to serve on boards and committees. I have occasionally seen businesses fail because their owners spent too much time serving on committees and boards that had nothing to do with their business. When I first started my business, a friend of mine, who also happened to be an elected official, asked me to serve on the board of a regional hospital. I was very flattered that he asked me to do this, and I quickly accepted his offer.

But during the confirmation process, I met with the chairman of the hospital board. He explained that the board met once a month, and that each board member was expected to chair at least one committee and to serve on at least one additional committee. I added up the time required for me to fulfill these obligations and found that I would be spending approximately thirty-five hours a month on activities related to the hospital board. Multiplied by twelve months, that would equal about 420 hours or about *eighteen days per year!* Taken over a ten year period, that would equal about *six months* that I was giving up to serve on this hospital board!

I also noticed that most of the other board members were retired, and therefore had much more available time than I did to serve on the board and its various committees. I quickly apologized and resigned from the board. It might have been an interesting experience (not to mention a positive boost to the ego) to serve on this hospital board. But ultimately, every hour I would have spent serving on hospital board business would have meant one hour away from my own business. It would have diverted me from what I needed to be doing, which was building my business and getting it into a sustainable mode.

> **Often, it's the things that you *don't* do in business, rather than the things that you do, that will determine whether or not you will succeed over the long haul.**

Again, you have to think long and hard about whether a commitment of your time will directly benefit your business, or whether it will only serve as a distraction and take you away from what you need to be doing. Often, it's the things that you *don't* do in business, rather than the things that you do, that will determine whether or not you will succeed over the long haul.

FRANCHISES

Franchises are a different kind of partnership, but one that seems to have a higher success rate than partnerships between friends and business associates. With franchises, you are partnering with a local or national company, instead of another person. Most are food franchises, followed by tanning salons, weight-loss programs, home services, cleaning, glass repair, and printing companies. Two-thirds of reporting franchises have been in business for twelve years or more. Retail food franchises seem to have the longest duration. Economic downturns result in an increase in franchises.

The advantage of a franchise is that it provides an established formula, and in many cases, is built on a strong brand name. Franchises are prepackaged like modular homes, and customers go to franchises because they like the familiarity. If you walk into a Subway restaurant in Grand Rapids, Michigan, you will get the same food as you would in a Subway in Grand Forks, North Dakota, or in the Subway in Grand Central Station in New York. And the interiors of these restaurants look pretty much the same, no matter where you go. Franchise owners typically have to do very little marketing to promote their business. Since I believe that many businesses fail because of a limited knowledge of marketing, franchises can be valuable for this reason alone.

But buying into a franchise also means that you are beholden to the parent company. Your success is limited by the demand for your particular franchise in your area and by your employees' ability to do their job well. I recommend that, prior to partnering with any franchise, you should try starting a business on your own. If you follow the principles outlined in this book—keeping low overhead, trusting your instincts, testing your concepts, etc.—you may be able to create a successful independent business. Then, if you wish, you can partner with a franchise in the future. Not only will you have experience in the business, you will also be in a position to negotiate what you need from the franchise and to eliminate what you don't need.

Before making any franchise agreement, talk to franchise owners in your area who have franchises similar to the one you are thinking of buying. Find out how well their particular franchise has done in your area and how successful their relationship has been with the parent company. Make sure you have a good business attorney look over the franchise agreement before you sign it.

Keep in close communication with the parent company from which you buy the franchise. But be cautious! Don't automatically assume that *everything* they tell you about how to set up and run your franchise is necessarily true or correct. Obviously, their formula for success has been duplicated many times. But when your gut instinct tells you that the parent company is wrong, *trust your gut instinct!*

I have a friend named Sally who bought into a printing franchise about ten years ago. She decided to open a print shop when she noticed a shortage of qualified printers in her immediate area. She heard that a national print chain was expanding to the West Coast. The printing chain required a hefty down payment with high monthly consulting fees, so Sally took out a second mortgage on her home and partnered with them.

The printing chain recommended a location about ten miles south of the community where Sally had envisioned the need for a print shop. Sally didn't understand the choice of the location but decided to trust the chain's recommendation. After all, they were the experts. She was sure the national chain had good reasons for selecting this location, such as foot traffic, easy access for surrounding businesses, etc.

But after the doors opened at her new print shop, Sally quickly learned that there were other highly competitive print shops in the immediate area. She had signed a long-term lease agreement with a high monthly rent, but the customer base just wasn't there. When she needed assistance, the national printing chain offered very little help. They didn't have a strong market presence in the first place, and it was expensive for them to send a representative out to the West Coast to help her.

In retrospect, Sally should have trusted her instincts, in spite of the national chain's recommendation. She should have looked for inexpensive retail space in the area where she first saw the need for a print shop. Instead of a long-term lease, she could have signed a six-month lease with an option to renew for three to five years. She could have then leased used printing equipment and supplied her future clients with very basic printing needs. By keeping her overhead low and testing her concept slowly, she could have stayed in business long enough to find out whether or not the print shop could work in the location that she had chosen.

Because Sally knew the neighborhood (and because she has a great personality and is very efficient), she could have gone door-to-door and personally met with her future clients. After several months, Sally would have known if the location for the print shop would be successful. She could then have extended her lease and upgraded the printing equipment over time.

If, after several months, Sally discovered that she had made a mistake in location, or if the customer base wasn't there to sustain a printing business, she could have shut down the operation and returned the leased printing equipment with minimal financial loss. She would now know a lot more about the printing business and could have made another go of it in another location. With a short lease, she could have moved quickly.

Unfortunately, after losing a ton of money with her print shop, Sally was forced to close her doors and declare bankruptcy. However, I'm happy to report that she has since landed on her feet and is now stronger than ever. It turned out that many of her clients at the print shop had a need for a graphic artist. Since Sally has a talent in this area, she started doing graphics work on the side. When the print shop closed, she had a client base to launch a graphics design firm. In recent years, she has expanded her business to provide clients with reproductions of graphic art from 18th century books.

The bad experience of my friend Sally might not be typical of franchises. Many franchise owners would probably tell you that they are very satisfied with their businesses. While franchises may provide a different business model than self-employment, the franchise owner can still benefit from applying the principles outlined in this book. Keeping overhead low, testing your concepts, and trusting your business instincts will help your business to prosper in the long run, and can help you to escape disasters, no matter what type of business you have.

(NOTE: Some information from the previous section was taken from an article on franchises by Alf Nucifora, an Atlanta-based marketing consultant. The article appeared in Puget Sound Business Journal, May 17, 2002, page 27. Alf Nucifora is a syndicated columnist who specializes in brilliant strategies for small business development at all levels. His syndicated columns can be found at his web site, www.nucifora.com.)

CHAPTER TWELVE

Marketing

I believe the number one reason that most businesses fail is that their owners do not understand marketing. If, as they say, "A little knowledge can be a dangerous thing," then the business owner who does not understand marketing is the one who knows just enough to be dangerous.

When it comes to marketing, many business owners simply assume that "anyone can do it." Often, they have no idea how to market or promote their enterprise. Successful marketing involves much more than just placing an ad in the local newspaper. And while you don't need a huge budget to advertise your product or service, it helps if you have an understanding of the basic principles of marketing.

When you start a small business, you should allocate a minimum of 7 to 10 percent of your annual budget for marketing purposes. For self-employed business owners, the most effective marketing tools haven't changed at all. Spend your time cold-calling prospective clients, sending out business cards and e-mails, and trying to get people to visit your web site. Go directly to the people who will help you to succeed.

You can also join networking groups and service clubs to market and promote your business, but be selective of the groups you join. The problem with networking groups is that *everyone* there is trying to sell something. Stay away from "feel-good" organizations that have general themes (e.g., "Gee, it's great to be a small business owner"). The only networking groups that are worthwhile, at least in the developing stages of your business, are those that will bring business directly to your company— that is, those that will put you in direct contact with potential clients or with people who know potential clients. Include the time that you personally spend networking in your annual marketing budget. If you are worth $85 per hour and you attend a two-hour chamber of commerce meeting to promote your business, this means that you have spent $170 on marketing.

There is no one single approach to marketing that will work for all types of businesses. But there are some basic principles for successful marketing. Understanding these principles will help you to promote your business more effectively. The four key principles are **consistency, simplicity, target,** and **execution**.

CONSISTENCY

Many businesses believe that a huge advertising budget is necessary to "get the word out," or they think it is essential to "brand" their products or services. They spend thousands of dollars on super-creative ad campaigns when a small, well-thought-out, and *consistent* marketing campaign will be much more effective. In whatever market you choose, you must *establish a consistent presence* for your business. *A long-term, consistent approach to marketing is much more cost-effective and will achieve a greater impact for your business than a huge, all-or-nothing one-time ad campaign.*

The trick is to find the right marketing medium for your business. I have seen many companies bounce around from one medium to another, unable to find the "one that works"— because they never stick with one medium long enough to see consistent results from it. For example, they might start out with direct mail. If they don't get an enormous response to their first mailing, they conclude that direct mail doesn't work. So they switch to running a newspaper ad. After several weeks, the ad still hasn't produced the response they wanted, so they cancel it. Then they might try a radio commercial. Once more, the medium doesn't produce as much of a response as they expected, so they decide that radio doesn't work.

> **There are over 11,000 commercial radio stations in the United States that are supported solely by advertising. Radio *must* be working for somebody!**

You see the problem? People who don't understand marketing often blame the medium if it doesn't meet their expectations. It's like blaming the messenger for delivering bad news. All of the above mediums work, including radio. There are over 11,000 commercial radio stations in the United States that are supported solely by advertising. Radio *must* be working for somebody!

It may be that radio advertising is *not* the most cost-effective medium for your business. When I encounter business people who say they want to "try a radio ad," I usually advise against it. In just a few seconds, I can see that radio is not their best marketing option. I may advise them to take a more local approach (e.g., a local newspaper, direct mail, a web site, and/ or the Yellow Pages). I then suggest that, after they get up and running and have expanded their business to several locations, they may want to consider coming back to me, and *then* we can talk about radio.

Every marketing medium works for *somebody*. It's up to you to figure out which medium (or mediums) will work best for you and stick with them. You must achieve *consistency* with your medium before you can effectively measure its results. Let's say you are an accountant and you want to send out a direct mail piece notifying the community of your services. It's obvious that a good direct mail house can help you to create an effective mailing piece and determine your target audience based on the services you offer. What isn't so obvious is the *frequency* that you should use for this or any other medium.

Never make a judgement on whether or not a certain medium works based on a frequency of one. If you send out one mailing and receive little response, *send it out again!* Decide at the beginning of the process how many times you will use a certain medium, and stick to that frequency.

For example, you may decide to send out the direct mail piece once a month, or once every other month. I believe that a six-month to one-year trial period is the minimum required before you can make an intelligent judgement as to whether or not your direct mail piece is working.

Here are some other tips to keep in mind for marketing consistency:

- Market early. If you are opening a restaurant or any business, start your promotions six months before you open your doors. Don't wait until the week before you open to start advertising.

- Even if, after a certain time period, your chosen medium does not seem to work, you should still stick with it for the predetermined length of time (e.g., one year). For example, if you are getting minimal response after three direct mailings, it could be that the *message* needs overhauling. Take a good look at your mailing and see if there might be some defect in the presentation of your message or a more effective way to state that message.

- Don't be unrealistic about the anticipated response. If you send out 100 direct mail pieces and you get two legitimate leads from the first mailing, *this is an excellent return.* Your response should build over time.

Many businesses make the mistake of having unrealistic expectations when it comes to marketing. For example, I once developed a radio ad campaign for a consulting firm that specialized in helping start-up businesses. This company offered a $7,500 business package that they claimed could help your start-up business to succeed if you followed their basic business principles.

I put together a proposal for a radio ad campaign for this company that cost a total of $2,500. I was being extremely conservative with my recommendations. I didn't want to run up a huge budget. I felt that if this very minimum radio campaign was successful, we could increase the presence at a later date. One week after the first commercials aired, I heard that this company had received forty-five inquiries as a result of the radio campaign. I was ecstatic! Forty-five calls from small business owners seeking a business package that would cost them $7,500 sounded like an excellent response to me. After all, we were not selling $15 CD's here, but a high-cost, esoteric service.

Let's do a little math. If the company could convert all forty-five inquiries into clients, they would gross $337,500 with a $2,500 investment! But this is being unrealistic. Obviously all forty-five would not convert into clients. However, if they managed to convert even *five* of those inquiries into clients, they would still gross $37,500. I considered this to be a great return. Just think what would be possible if this company continued with the radio commercials over several months as part of a consistent marketing plan?

Unfortunately, the client didn't see it that way. They felt that forty-five inquiries was not enough and decided not to do any further radio-based ad campaigns. I was absolutely stunned. I felt that this was the best marketing job I had ever done for a client and that I had delivered everything that was promised.

What I didn't count on was a client who was not educated about marketing and, more important, about expectations. In retrospect I should have sat down with the client beforehand and established advanced parameters for what they could have expected from the radio campaign. By letting the client know what they could *realistically* expect, and by mapping out a strategy that would allow them to establish a *consistent presence* using the campaign, I might have persuaded the client to stick with the campaign long enough to prove its effectiveness.

SIMPLICITY

We've all heard the quote: *"Keep it simple, stupid!"* No truer words were ever spoken or written, particularly when it comes to marketing.

It is estimated that an average person receives over 10,000 messages a day. From morning to night, we are bombarded with ads and messages trying to sell us something. We can't walk down the street, turn on our computers, or even fill up our gas tanks without being pitched some new product or service. People have become so *accustomed* to being swamped with marketing messages that they rarely give advertisements a second look. Therefore, it is *absolutely essential* that your audience should understand your marketing messages *at first glance.*

Start with a simple name for your business that tells people *exactly* what your company does. If you have a slogan, it should sum up your services and/or target audience in a few simple words. Here are some good examples:

- Safeguard Business Accounting: "Meeting the Needs of Small Businesses"

- Casey Communications Inc.: "Broadcast and Print: Creative, Production, & Placement"

- Oakbrook Dry Cleaning: "In by 8, out by 5"

This may seem perfectly obvious, but a surprising number of businesses fail to follow this basic marketing rule. Getting the name of your business right is the most important marketing decision that you will ever make.

Again, Webvan.com and HomeGrocer.com provide a perfect example. Anyone who had never heard of Webvan.com might assume that it was a web-based shipping or furniture moving company. No one could tell from its name that Webvan.com provided an online grocery service—a message that is completely obvious with a well-thought-out company name like HomeGrocer.com.

Here's another example of two companies that provide the exact same service. One company name tells you exactly what they do. The other does not.

- Guardian Security Systems: Commercial Access Systems

- Dolphin Technology Inc.

Guardian Security Systems declares in its name exactly what it does. The company even states in its headline that they serve commercial clients. On the other hand, one might assume from its name that Dolphin Technology is a high-tech oceanography research firm. Perhaps they produce locating devices that can be attached to dolphins to monitor their migration patterns. You would never guess from their name that they also specialize in security software.

> **Getting the name of your business right is the most important marketing decision that you will ever make.**

Even the logic of the name "Dolphin Technology" is fuzzy. What do dolphins have to do with providing security for computer networks? At least the name "Guardian Security Systems" gives you a clear metaphor. Their software product will serve as a guardian for your network, thus preventing hackers and spammers from breaking into it.

When people who do not understand marketing are evaluating the effectiveness of an advertising medium, the first question they often ask is "How many calls did you get from the advertisement?" The more pertinent question to ask is "How many *qualified* calls did you get from the advertisement?" In other words, how many calls did you get from the advertisement *from people or companies who might actually have a need to do business with you?*

Along these lines, can you imagine the number of unqualified calls that Guardian Security does *not* get because who they are and what their company does is *spelled out* in their name and subtitle? Can you imagine the number of time-wasting phone calls that Dolphin Technology receives from people who think that the company specializes in marine biology? Remember, time is your most precious resource as a business owner. You must preserve it any way you can, and one of the easiest ways is to avoid unwanted phone calls from people who will not be doing business with your company.

Law firms are the worst at promoting who they are and what they do. For example: *"Seather, Campbell, Olsen, Snelling, Hopkins, Riddell, Sessler, and Associates."*

All I see here are a bunch of names. It doesn't even say, "The Law Offices of" or tell you what kind of law they practice. Here are some better examples of law firms who got it right.

- Mussehl Personal Injury Law Firm

- Crowell Divorce Lawyers & Associates

- Jackson Intellectual Property Law Group

If you can't create a name for your enterprise that tells people exactly what your business is all about, you have made your first major marketing mistake. Furthermore, it is a mistake that will be very difficult and expensive to correct.

I speak from experience on this. When I first started my monthly newspaper, the name of my publication was *Maturing*. Since the newspaper was directed towards the aging population, I thought that the title correctly indicated my target audience. However, I didn't care for the title because it really didn't say anything other than, "You are getting older." (I figured my readers didn't need *me* to tell them this.)

I wanted to change the name of the publication, but I didn't know exactly what the change would be. I knew that if I were to make a change, I would have to really think it through and *stick* with that change once I'd made it. If I kept changing the name of my newspaper, my readers and advertisers would think that I didn't know what I was doing.

I had subtitled the newspaper "The Voice of Experience," because I wanted my readers to know that the articles featured in the publication were written by people with experience in their fields, and also that my readers were experienced people. After thinking for a long time about possible new titles for my publication, it suddenly hit me that "The Voice of Experience" expressed everything that I was trying to convey in the newspaper. The solution was literally right before my eyes.

It was time-consuming and expensive to make the transition from *Maturing* to *Voices of Experience*. I had to change the newspaper's masthead, print new business cards, letterhead, and envelopes, and redo all of the promotional materials. In the end, I think it was worth it. The readers and advertisers were supportive of the change but, most important, I felt really good about it. Still, I wish I had got it right the first time around.

If you take the time to come up with a simple and effective name for your business, other forms of marketing should fall into place. Always remember, keep your messages simple and direct.

If you create a name for your product, make sure that name reflects exactly what the product is or does. For example, for a long time I considered naming this book, *Flying Under the Clouds*.

I thought this was a good metaphor for the lessons I was trying to teach in this book. To survive as a business owner, you must learn how to "fly under the clouds," so to speak. You must keep your business small and simple, keep your overhead low, be organized and timely, etc., in order to avoid the "clouds," or trouble spots, that can plague small businesses. I dropped the title *Flying Under the Clouds* when I realized that people might think it was a book about aviation. (I listened to my own advice. Don't make it hard for your customers or clients to find you.)

Then I started to think about using the title *Sustaining a Business in the 21st Century*. I thought this was appropriate, because I was trying to teach people not just how to *start* a business, but also how to *keep it going over the long run.* Gradually, however, I realized that this book was more about personality traits and survival for the *self-employed* business owner. Also, the word "sustaining" might imply that this was a book for people who have already started their business. Eventually, my publisher and I decided on the title *Is Self-Employment for You?*, with the subtitle *"Anyone can start a business…only a few can sustain a business."* (Now that you have read a good part of the book, I hope it is about what you expected from the title.)

One last word about naming your business. If you have a truly innovative product or service, don't get caught in the trap of trying to establish a brand name over your competitors. In the late 1990's, many of the dot-coms spent millions of dollars trying to be the first to brand their product or service. Their strategy was to discourage potential competitors from entering into the marketplace by establishing themselves as the "original" web-based bookseller, groceries seller, etc. In 1999 and 2000, 60 percent of all radio advertising budgets in major markets were from dot-coms trying to "brand" themselves.

Don't try to fight the inevitable. Remember, you can copyright a brand name, but not a product or service. Any successful business concept will eventually be duplicated. McDonald's introduced the concepts of speed, cleanliness, efficiency, and consistency of product in serving fast food; these concepts were then copied by Burger King, Wendy's, and a dozen others. Starbucks was the prototype for the "fast-food coffee store," and its concept has since been duplicated by Tully's and many other espresso coffee shops. If you succeed in inventing or developing an original product or service, someone else will try to copy your idea. Don't spend even one second worrying about it. Worry first about making a profit, not about capturing market share for your business.

TARGET

Finding your target audience is a critical component of any marketing plan. Again, this may sound obvious, but I have known too many businesses that did not understand their target market.

Here's an example. Several years ago, I approached an independent retirement community that had just opened for business. I was still publishing my newspaper at the time, and my radio show was going strong. I considered this retirement center a good potential client for advertising. They turned me down at first. Like many business owners in the long-term retirement industry, they believed that the market would come to them.

> **Worry first about making a profit, not about capturing market share for your business.**

Six months later, they called me back. I discovered that the facility itself was almost empty of residents and the management had recently fired their marketing director. Once again, they had killed the messenger. They hadn't given the marketing director any advertising budget to work with, but they had expected the facility to be filled within weeks of its opening.

In meeting with the owner, I asked him what he considered to be the target market for his facility. When he said that it was people aged sixty to seventy, I almost fell off my chair. My experience with this industry had taught me that the demographic age group for retirement centers was *much* higher, perhaps people in their late seventies to early eighties.

The owner obviously wanted to target a younger demographic, so that the turnover of residents would not be as great. This was an "independent retirement" community, meaning that the retirement center offered no assisted living or heavy care programs. If you were going to live in this particular community, you had to be independent and healthy. Assisted living communities, adult family homes, and nursing homes filled the long-term care needs for the most frail of the aging population.

The owner kept insisting that sixty- to seventy-year-olds were his target market. "There *has* to be something wrong with the marketing plan," he told me, "if you can't convince a sixty-five-year-old to move in here."

Then I asked him how old *he* was.

He said sixty-seven. I asked him if he would be willing to give up his home and move into his own retirement community. He admitted that he would not. He finally got the point, and the target demographic for the community was raised to around eighty years old.

For an independent retirement community, the primary target market is the person in their late seventies or early eighties who is still in good health and capable of making the decision to move in. I would say that the average age of a resident living at this particular retirement community was around eighty-two. I would also estimate that the average resident would live there for five to seven years before they need additional care available at another facility. That is more turnover than the owner would have liked, but that's how it goes when a retirement facility does not offer additional care programs.

At the meeting, the owner and I discussed a number of promotional opportunities for the community, most of which were eventually implemented. I'm pleased to say that within six months after we began to market the retirement community towards the correct target market, the facility was full and plans for a second building were underway.

So it is very important to know your specific target market. As another example, it is not enough to say that you are targeting a "young adult market." Do you mean college-educated young adults? Or young adults who have just graduated from high school within the past two years? Do you primarily want to target a male or female audience? Is your major target age group eighteen to twenty-four, or twenty-five to twenty-nine, or thirty to thirty-seven? It is no longer enough to say that you are targeting the eighteen to forty-nine demographic. In today's market, an eighteen-year-old adult has virtually nothing in common with a forty-nine-year-old adult.

Make sure you have a clear and precise idea of your primary and secondary markets. Often, you have to peel the onion down to its core to find out who your true clients or customers are. If you take the time to probe deeper, you may discover that your true market is not what you thought it was.

EXECUTION

You can be the smartest individual on the planet, but unless you effectively execute your brainstorm or concept, you have absolutely nothing. I can create the best radio spot ever recorded, but unless it gets to the radio station on time and with the right phone numbers for the customer to call, the spot itself is worth zero to the client. The most effective marketing plan is the one that gets implemented correctly and on time.

More people fail than succeed in the execution of their marketing plans. I can't tell you the number of times that I have seen great pamphlets, brochures, and publications sent out to thousands of people *with the wrong contact address or phone number!* It does not do your business any good if your potential clients or customers can't call you or find your business. A mistake like this can even make your potential clients reluctant to work with you. After all, if you can't even get the right address or phone number on your brochure or flyer, how can they trust you to provide *them* with a good product or service? (I encountered this kind of mistake more frequently when I was working in government service, but I have seen it made by a number of private businesses as well.)

One story that comes to mind personally happened when I was publishing my monthly newspaper. When I mailed out my newspaper, I used a mailing house, run by a free agent, to handle the labeling and distribution. This particular mailing house had a good track record with me and did an admirable job of getting my publication out on time with very few problems. However, after one slightly negative experience with them, I decided to try using one of their competitors who had been calling me frequently to find out if I would be interested in using their services.

Almost every issue of a newspaper or magazine is time-sensitive, meaning that the issue *must* arrive in the mailboxes of its readers on or before a certain date. Usually, this is because some of the advertisers are promoting a special event in the publication. If the issue is received on the day before, or worse on the day *after* the event, the ad is of no value to the advertiser. This makes it very important for the publisher to deliver the newspaper or magazine to the mailing house in time for them to label the publication and get it to the post office for an on-time mailing.

In this particular issue of my newspaper, I had a whole section dedicated to an upcoming employment fair for older adults. I had sold advertising for the issue to many of the companies who were participating in the employment fair, and I hoped that some of my readers would attend. I had an agreement with the account executive at the mailing house that if the newspapers were delivered by 9 AM on Thursday morning, they would be labeled and delivered to the post office that afternoon.

I met the deadline. The newspapers were delivered to the mailing house by 8:45 AM. I was talking to the account executive on the phone as the newspapers arrived at their warehouse. He assured me once again that they would be labeled and delivered to the post office that very afternoon.

One way I monitored the mailing of my newspaper was to have an issue mailed to my home address. Even though the newspaper was normally mailed out using bulk mail, I usually received the newspaper either the very next day or two days after it was delivered to the post office. The employment fair was taking place on the following Friday, so most of my readers should have received the paper almost a week in advance.

But I didn't receive the newspaper the following day, nor did I receive it on Saturday. The following Monday was a federal holiday, so there would be no mail delivery at all. When I didn't receive my newspaper in the mail on Tuesday, I immediately called the account executive at the mail house. He informed that the newspapers hadn't been mailed yet! My newspapers were now going to be of little value to the companies who had advertised in my paper in hopes of drawing people to the employment fair. I won't put into print what I told the account executive during our phone conversation, but that was the end of our relationship. I quickly went back to using my previous mailing house.

On a side note, this is one of those times when it's important to be absolutely accountable with your clients. After my bad experience with the new mailing house, I personally called all the clients who had advertised in my newspaper for the employment fair. I told them exactly what had happened and took full responsibility. (Yes, the mailing house had screwed up, but I was the one who had hired them.) I explained to each client the circumstances surrounding the late delivery, and told them that they were under no obligation to pay for their ad in the newspaper. As it turned out, **all** of my advertisers were very sympathetic to what had happened and paid for their ads anyway.

Again, the lesson here is that you can put a great deal of work into a marketing project but unless it is properly executed, your efforts will be wasted. *Execution is not only important in marketing, it is also an extremely critical element to the long-term survival of your business.*

A WORD ABOUT CREATIVITY

We have all observed incredibly creative advertising campaigns on television, on the radio, in print, and in numerous other communications outlets. If you can be both creative and effective in marketing your products or services, more power to you. But there is such a thing as being *too* creative.

After I have watched a humorous or "edgy" television commercial or listened to a radio spot with someone else, I make a point of asking that person at the end of the commercial "Who was the advertiser?" The commercial may have been a creative masterpiece, but many times when I ask that question, the person doesn't have a clue as to what company was being promoted. This means the commercial has failed. I have seen too many advertising agencies that are more concerned about winning a creative trophy at an end-of-the-year awards banquet than they are about getting results for the client.

AFLAC Insurance is an example of a company that has the right mix of a creative theme and the frequency to make it work. Who hasn't seen the series of commercials with the duck continuing to brand the name "AFLAC" around clueless human beings? What makes the AFLAC commercial series so effective is that the duck keeps *repeating* the company name in all the commercials. The company has remained consistent with this series of commercials and has invested millions of dollars over several years in making sure that the message sinks in. When the series first started, I saw the first AFLAC duck commercial at least ten times before it really started to take hold.

Now compare the AFLAC ads with another commercial series. This series features a sleek silver sports car or SUV, speeding down the interstate and through city streets, while a background chorus chants, "Zoom, zoom, zoom!" Eventually, the car passes a little boy in a black suit who is standing by the side of the road. The boy looks at the camera and whispers cryptically, "Zoom, zoom!"

All very creative and eye-catching. But think about this: *Can you remember the name of the car brand that is being advertised with this series of commercials?*

Most people can't. All they remember is the "Zoom, zoom, zoom" chant and the weird little boy at the end of the commercial. (The car brand, by the way, is Mazda.)

And therein lies the problem with most super-humorous creative ads. They don't follow the four basic principles of marketing, which must work together *as a whole* for an ad campaign to be successful. There may be a flaw in the execution of the ad campaign (as when Mazda fails to put their brand name in the "Zoom, zoom" chant). Or perhaps the advertiser doesn't back up the creative ads with the frequency and longevity needed to make the campaign work. As soon as the audience is beginning to "get it," the advertising budget for the campaign has already been exhausted.

The point is, you should never assume that being creative or funny will give you an advantage in advertising your business. Unless you have a huge advertising budget, I strongly recommend that you stick with the basics in advertising your product or services. Resist the temptation to be too funny or indirect with your promotional efforts, no matter what medium you choose to advertise in. *Super-creative advertising means nothing if your potential clients or customers remember the advertisement, but can't remember the name of your business or what you offer.*

AWARDS

I am not a big believer in seeking awards from associations or organizations. Awards supposedly validate your business. They may give you visibility, standing, or a stamp of approval, but the fact is, they are forgotten after the evening is over. There is also the chance that you will make the fatal mistake of believing your own press releases and begin to rest on your laurels.

You cannot allow yourself to rest on yesterday's successes. Like life, business is a continuous process that never ends. It will be remembered that you performed well for a client, but you will be expected to duplicate and improve upon those results for all the clients that follow. As in baseball, your success in business is not necessarily measured by your last hit, but by how you perform on your next time at bat.

As Donny Deutsch, CEO of Deutsch, once said, *"Creative awards are immaterial and stupid because great work is work that moves your business."*

CHAPTER THIRTEEN

Keeping Your Overhead Low

When you become a self-employed business owner, keeping your expenses at an absolute minimum is essential for the survival of your business. As we've already seen, many businesses fail because their overhead is just too high. The dot-coms in particular were notorious for losing hundreds of millions of dollars because they didn't have the slightest concern or discipline for controlling their money. Their losses were equated to a "burn rate." If you are self-employed, a burn rate is the equivalent of watching your business go up in smoke.

Be absolutely ruthless in hanging on to every dollar you own. Again, before you make any huge purchases, ask yourself how much your business really *needs* what you are buying and whether or not you can get along without it. Look around for bargains. Check secondhand stores and outlets for low-priced office furniture, look around at surplus houses for used computers and electronic equipment, and try to buy office supplies wholesale. Let the big boys sit in the glass towers, drive expensive cars, and strategize about how and when to launch an IPO. By limiting your expenditures to *necessities* and avoiding *luxuries* as you build your business, you can avoid the trouble spots that often plague start-ups.

Keeping your overhead low doesn't mean being cheap. It just means knowing how to spend your money wisely and where to invest. For example, it is critical that you have a good appearance when you meet with potential clients or customers. You don't have to spend $2,500 on a business suit, but you shouldn't spend $99 either. Instead, you could spend $650 to $850 on two or three high-quality suits rather than five cheap suits.

GETTING STARTED

How much money do you really need to start your business? It depends on what type of business you start. My best advice is to make a list of the bare minimum you will need to get your business going, and stick to list. Do not make any huge investments to build your business until you know if it is going to work or not.

I had about $20,000 when I started my business fifteen years ago. One reason I started out as a publisher was that publishing didn't require a huge cash outlay up-front. I didn't need to sign a long-term lease agreement for equipment or office space. The success of my newspaper rested largely on my imagination for strong editorial content and on my ability to sell advertising. If I'd found that I wasn't able to cut it in either department, I could have easily shut the business down with minimal loss.

Before you start your business, it is best to make sure that your personal expenses will be taken care of, as well as your business expenses. If you decide to quit your job, it is a good idea to have enough money saved to cover about six months' worth of expenses before taking the plunge into full-time entrepreneurship. Even if your spouse works and has agreed to support the family while you are building your business, it is best to have money in reserve to cover your expenses in case something should go wrong (e.g, your spouse loses their job or is suddenly no longer able to work).

FINANCING: FORGET BANKS

You'll notice that I've saved financing your business for the last part of the book. I have discussed financing in relation to partnerships and keeping your overhead low, but what about getting the necessary financing to keep your business going?

If you think that banks will help you to finance your business, think again. With banks, the general rule is: *If you need the money, it's not available. If you don't need the money, bank lenders will break down your door trying to lend it to you.*

Banks treat small business owners like second-class citizens. They don't trust us because we don't have a "traditional job," meaning an eight-to-five office job with a regular, predetermined salary. It doesn't matter if you have been in business for fifteen years, are making excellent profits, and have a stellar credit history. If you try to borrow money, bank lenders look at you as if you have some kind of infectious disease.

In the last three years, I have earned three times as much income as my wife. Yet banks still consider *her* to be the main breadwinner of the household because she works for a large company and has a "real job." In my opinion, a person who has run a business successfully for an extended period of time is less of a risk than someone who has a so-called "steady job." An entrepreneur can be very resourceful in making payments to their billers and creditors when the money gets tight. Someone who loses a steady or secure job is like a deer in the headlights. They freeze and think that their whole world has suddenly come to an end.

But banks don't see it that way. In their minds, if you are a small business owner, the failure of your business is just around the corner. (After all, you could walk out the bank door and have an anvil drop on your head.)

Not that I am bitter about this, you understand.

If you wish to finance your own business, your best options are:

- A loan from a relative.

- Money from your own personal savings account.

- A second mortgage on your home. Banks will always give you a second mortgage on property you own, although they may charge you a slightly higher interest rate if you are self-employed.

THE DANGERS OF HAVING TOO MUCH MONEY

If not understanding marketing is the number one reason why businesses fail, having too much money is a close second. Many start-up businesses suffer from the curse of being overcapitalized, rather than undercapitalized. They have too much money in the beginning, rather than too little.

The problem with having too much money when you start a business is that you feel obliged to do more, be more, spend more, grow faster. You feel as if you should maximize your business, make it as big as possible, when in fact you should be keeping your business and its expenditures at an absolute minimum until you establish yourself. Again, the dot-coms were notorious for having too much capital. They spent themselves into oblivion while trying to establish themselves as big names on the Internet frontier.

You might think that having too much money is the last thing a small business owner would need to worry about, but I have seen entrepreneurs fail in their ventures for exactly this reason. About the time I started my business, a colleague of mine started her own public relations firm. She opened her doors with beautiful offices in a prime location and had a good-sized staff to help launch her business. I knew that her father was quite wealthy and that he was financing most of her start-up costs.

I'll admit I was a bit jealous of her at the time. Again, I started my own business in a one-person office located in a building owned by the printers who printed my newspaper. I was constantly struggling to stay in business, making cold calls to clients and selling advertising to pay for the next issue of my paper. I would have given anything to have the financial resources that my colleague had.

I fully expected her public relations firm to be successful. She was (and is) an extremely bright person and was well-connected in the community. Prior to starting my newspaper, I had used her firm for public relations purposes while I was working on a volunteer project for a small organization.

But, once more, her problem turned out to be too much overhead. I don't know exactly what her expenses were on a monthly basis, but they had to be quite high. Office rent was at least $5,000-7,000 per month. Add another $15,000 in salaries for her employees, and you can see the trouble coming. If her overhead was, at a minimum, $20,000 per month, that comes to $240,000 over twelve months in the first year! Not long after she started her business, a recession set in and there weren't too many new clients around who were looking for public relations work. As you can probably guess, her business soon folded.

In the years since this happened, I have learned a lot about running a business. Looking back, I think I might have been lucky, in a way, not to start out with a ton of money to finance my entrepreneurship. I think if I'd had the same financial resources as my colleague, I might have done exactly what she did. That is, I might have started my own small business with a few employees, high-profile office space, and lots of expenses. And

I might very well have *lost* that same business later on, when those expenses started to get out of hand.

As it was, I started out with very little money and had to work very hard to keep my business going. In the long run, this turned out to be a blessing. I have known several entrepreneurs whose lives were *too* easy, and who therefore did not feel that they had to work as hard to make their businesses succeed. In the end, this may have cost them their businesses.

A LITTLE FEAR CAN BE A GOOD THING

As I mentioned in Chapter Ten, when I first started my business, there was another publisher in the office next door to mine who was publishing his own bimonthly newspaper. This publisher's business soon folded because he spent too much time working on his computer and not enough time making sales calls to potential advertisers for his paper. While I believe that lack of organization was one of the major reasons his business failed, I think that was only part of it.

This publisher happened to be married to a very wealthy spouse who was a highly paid executive at one of Seattle's most famous corporations. And while the publisher wasn't a freeloader (prior to starting his own business, he himself had been a successful executive), the fact that he had other financial resources meant that he didn't have to worry as much about the success or failure of his business. If his business failed, he would still have food on the table.

Because of his shared wealth, this publisher lost an important incentive to succeed: Fear! He would come in late to the office, and would leave early. I never once saw him come in and work on the weekends. On the other hand, I was single and didn't have a lot of money to fall back on. Therefore, I had a *major* incentive to succeed. I worked longer hours and came in to work on the weekends out of a pure need to keep eating and to pay my rent.

While it's certainly best to start a business when you have another source of steady income (e.g., support from your spouse), a little fear can be a good thing. Those who worry about the success or failure of their business have an advantage in that they are inclined to try harder, do better, and work longer hours to ensure that their business survives. As my friend Larry Coffman would often say, that *"knot in your gut"* isn't necessarily a bad thing.

OFFICE SPACE

Many people ask me whether or not a self-employed business owner should have a home office. I don't think there is an absolute yes or no answer to this question. If you are in a business where the primary function is to exchange information—for example, if you are an accountant, graphic designer, lawyer, publisher, software developer, Internet provider, etc.—a home office is preferable in the beginning because it keeps your overhead low. The main disadvantage of a home office is the isolation. A home office can be very lonely, particularly if you enjoy human interaction.

I can't stress enough the importance of treating a home office as if it were a regular office, located in an office building. You should have a separate room for your office, set apart from the rest of your house or apartment. Even if your office is next to your bedroom, put the name of your business on the door and lock it up at night. Make sure all the members of your family know that this is a place of business, not a place where they can sit at your desk and play computer games or surf the Internet. See the "Further Reading" section at the end of this book for a listing of books on how to start a successful business from a home office.

If you reach the point in your business where renting office space becomes a necessity, try to look around for an affordable office in a good, well-maintained location. Do not sign a long-term lease. Try to find a lease that will allow you a trial period (e.g., six months) to see if the office and location work for you, with an option to renew for an extended period. Make sure that your office is as close to your house as possible, so that your commute will be short and easy.

When I started my business, I got lucky when it came to office space. I learned the publishing business from Larry Coffman, one of the finest publishers in the country, and who taught me many of the principles contained in this book. Larry negotiated free office space for my small publishing company in the building owned by the printing company that published our newspapers. My first office was not glamorous, but it was very functional and it was free. This arrangement lasted several years and probably saved me over $100,000 in rent, electricity, office maintenance, parking, etc.

However, there is a point when this type of an arrangement can become counterproductive. In my case, employees at the printing company that owned the building where I had my office started taking our print jobs for granted. They viewed our small-press newspapers as being secondary to clients who were paying them $100,000 a year in printing bills. If one of their high-paying clients missed a press time, they would sometimes push *our* jobs back to accommodate the client. Their argument to us was "Why should you complain? We're giving you free office space!"

After a while, my free office space was not actually free. By taking the rent-free office, I was essentially giving up any negotiating leverage that I had with the printing company. As I've said before, newspaper publishing is a time-sensitive business, and it was more important for me to get my newspaper out on time than to have a free office. So I bought a one-bedroom condo in downtown Seattle and used it for my office for about six years. I found a new printing company that would take my small-press print jobs more seriously and with whom I could negotiate on more even terms.

Nothing is ever truly "free" in business. There is always a price to be paid, but sometimes you have to pay it. If you are supposedly getting something "free," or even at a discount, it's best to review that arrangement often and find out how much money you are *really* saving.

If you decide to lease office space, read your lease agreement *very* carefully. I don't wish to be offensive, but many property managers are not at the top of the food chain when it comes to ethics. They typically try to stack the deck in their favor in whatever contract you sign with them. I recently vacated an office in downtown Seattle after a property manager tried to horn-swoggle me. (And if you've ever had your horn swoggled, you know what a painful experience *that* can be.)

I had been in this particular office location for about three years, and it was almost time to renew my lease. During this three-year period, there was a high office vacancy rate in downtown Seattle. I thought the property manager for my office building would be anxious to keep me on and I could probably negotiate a better rent deal for myself on my lease renewal. When the property manager called me and left a voice-mail message about renewing my lease, I called back and left a message on his voice-mail saying that I was eager to extend the lease on my current office.

A few days later, the property manager called back and left another message on my voice-mail. He said he had already leased out my office to the business group next door to me, but that he had some other office space in the building that he would be glad to show me. Needless to say, I was stunned and angry! I couldn't believe that he had leased out my office to someone else without talking to me first.

I was also a bit relieved that I had found this out before any problems occurred. It might have been somewhat embarrassing for me if I had come to work one Monday morning to find that the business group next door had moved into my office over the weekend. ("Oh, hi, Mr. Casey. Uhh, we moved your computer desk and your bookshelves out into the hall. I assume the movers are coming today to pick up your stuff and take it to your new office?")

I found a new downtown office in another building and moved there as quickly and as quietly as possible. I didn't even bother to tell the property manager that I was vacating my old office. Later, when I took a good look at my old lease agreement, I discovered clauses in the contract stating that the property owners could order me to move out of my office at any time with sixty days notice. I also discovered a clause stating that, even with our negotiated rental agreement, the property owners could raise my rent any time they wished.

Be very, very careful when you lease office space. Always read your rental agreement in full and look for hidden clauses that would give your property manager an unfair advantage. If there is any part of your lease you don't understand, have an attorney look over the agreement before you sign it.

SURROUND YOURSELF WITH FREE AGENTS

When you start your own business, surround yourself with other free agents so you can *rent* their skills when you need them. When you don't need their skills any more, move on. This doesn't mean that you should *end* your relationship with other free agents once they have finished the job for which you hired them. You should, of course, keep in close contact with them in case you need their services in the future. My relationships with many of the free agents I work with go back to the very beginning of my business. But always remember that any business relationship you develop with a free agent is just that—a business relationship. Business is not about making friends; it's about cultivating colleagues.

Of course, if you make friends along the way, that's a bonus. Usually, however, the relationship continues only as long as both parties are benefiting financially. The relationship ends, in most cases, when that incentive goes away. In fifteen years of business, I have never hired any employees, and I never plan to. I do make a policy of paying free agents generously for the services they provide. I respect the people I work with and want to keep working with them for as long as possible.

> **Business is not about making friends; it's about cultivating colleagues.**

When you are looking to hire a free agent, the best person to hire is someone like yourself, who is sustaining their own business. Their mindset will be closest to yours. They know that if they don't give you their best work, you will move on to someone else who does. Free agents who run their own enterprise usually get the job done right the first time. If they don't, they are the ones who will stay up all night correcting their mistakes. The free agents who work with me know that I do not tolerate missed deadlines.

LET FREE AGENTS DO THE REPETITIVE WORK

As CEO of your company, it is your responsibility to create the systems that allow your business to run smoothly and efficiently. When you get to the point where you have a series of repetitive tasks that take you away from the more important aspects of your business, it is easy and cost-effective to hire free agents to handle those tasks for you.

The types of free agents you work with depend on the nature of your business. Again, when I was publishing my newspaper, I hired free agents to handle the repetitive tasks of editing and proofreading, and to input the weekly articles for my paper into my laptop computer. This freed up my time as CEO of the company to make sales calls and meet with potential advertisers.

Today, I use free agents to write, produce, record, sell, and distribute radio commercials for my clients. I use a free agent who specializes in voice-overs to narrate the radio commercials, and another free agent to provide sound effects. I even used a free agent to help me in writing this book, and another free agent to design the book cover. Once it is published, another free agent will help me to sell the book.

One of the very first free agents you should hire, no matter what type of business you have, is a good accountant. Don't be tempted by those web sites that allow you to prepare your tax returns over the Internet and send your forms directly to the IRS. A good tax accountant can save you a ton of money in business tax deductions. In the past fifteen years, my accountants have saved my business far more money than I've paid out for their services.

CHAPTER FOURTEEN

82% of Success is Showing Up

Woody Allen once said, *"80% of success is just showing up."* I have come to appreciate Mr. Allen's maxim for success more and more over the years. I've added two extra percentage points, because I think Mr. Allen's observation is so very important.

Here is what I think Woody Allen meant:

SHOWING UP EQUALS CONSISTENCY

a. The espresso-cart owner always opens for business at 7 AM, every day.

b. The architect's blueprint is delivered on time.

c. The athlete shows up for practice and to the game on time.

d. The salesperson shows up for an appointment on time.

e. An actor is on the set when filming begins.

f. The plumber pays his bills on time.

Showing up is the foundation for *sustaining* a business. You may not know it at the time, but starting a business is the *easy* part of the process. It's like planning for a wedding. A great deal of effort goes into making your wedding the perfect day. The bride has imagined this day her whole life. This is the one day that she will be the princess, and all eyes will be on her.

But too often, energies are directed toward the wedding day and the honeymoon. It's what happens *after* you get back from the honeymoon that determines whether or not the marriage will last. Your marriage will be much more successful if you show up for dinner at home every night after work and if you wake up next to your spouse every morning.

It's the same for running a business. When I first started in publishing, I had a hell of a time getting the first issue of my newspaper off the press. I was not meeting my sales goals, and I was having difficulty working with the page compositor for the layout of the first issue. Since selling advertising brought in the revenue for my paper, that seemed to be my most compelling challenge.

I visited a very successful publisher of a local newspaper group and talked with him about the problems I was having. I was surprised when he told me that getting the first newspaper out the door was the *easy* part. It was getting the *second*, the *third,* the *tenth*, and the *thirtieth* issue printed that would be the real challenge.

I soon learned he was right. When you are starting an enterprise, in my case a newspaper, you can rely on the good will of former colleagues, family, and friends to support you in your early efforts. About 30 percent of the advertising sales for my first issue was purchased by colleagues and friends. But after that enthusiasm wears off, *you are truly on your own!* In my case, I couldn't expect my friends and colleagues to buy advertising space in *every* issue of my newspaper. I had to go out and sell advertising to complete strangers, and *that* turned out to be the real challenge.

It's the same for almost any business. If you open a restaurant, the first night will be full of family and friends celebrating your grand opening. That enthusiasm and support may last for a couple of days. But how will your restaurant be doing six months from now? Only by "showing up," day after day—that is, going to work every day, providing your customers with good food and exceptional service, advertising regularly in local magazines, newspapers, and restaurant guides, and making adjustments to your menu or services if necessary—can you build a successful business and keep it going for the long term.

After talking with this publisher, I started to think seriously about the advertising sales and editorial content for the second, third, and fourth issues of my newspaper. If I hadn't listened to his advice, I would have been a one-issue publisher.

I should mention that this publisher did me another big favor. He told me I was going to fail! "I've seen your type before, young man. You're enthusiastic, but very naïve. You've got no idea what the newspaper business is *really* like. My advice is that you don't go into publishing at all."

For some reason, this advice galvanized me, and I was more determined than ever to make the newspaper succeed. I wanted to prove this publisher wrong. When times got tough, I would remember what he had said, and it made me more determined to make my publication work. As a result, I continued to "show up" for my newspaper. I was in my office every day, making cold calls to potential advertisers and checking the editorial content. I printed the second issue, and the third, and the fifth, and the one hundredth. My newspaper lasted for eight years, thanks to this publisher's advice.

(Often, when you read about very successful people in various walks of life, you find that many of them were driven by some *negative* energy. It might be the coach who tells the basketball player, "You're too short to make the team." Or it might be the teacher who tells the student, "You'll never get into law school." In many cases, such as mine, this only makes people more determined to succeed.)

EXECUTION: MAKING IT HAPPEN

Execution was stressed in marketing. I want to stress it again here as being an incredibly important ingredient for the success of your overall business.

Thomas Edison said it best: *"1 percent inspiration; 99 percent perspiration."* I now know what he meant. Mr. Edison was the father of many inventions, with the electric light bulb being the most famous. It took several years of overcoming setbacks before Thomas Edison finally got the masses to see the light (pun intended).

Thomas Edison said it best: *"1 percent inspiration; 99 percent perspiration."* By the time he invented the light bulb, Thomas Edison was already famous for having invented a number of other useful devices, including the phonograph. With the backing of investors like J.P. Morgan, Edison set out to invent an incandescent lamp that would run on electrical power. After Edison created his initial design for the light bulb, he assembled a team of scientists and electrical engineers to help him in his laboratory in Menlo Park, New Jersey.

The first step was to have a glass blower blow a glass bulb that could be used as the basis for the lamp. For each experiment, Edison would insert a filament wire inside the bulb, then seal the bulb and vacuum the air out of it. His engineers would then hook the bulb up to a portable generator, turn on the electrical power, and hope for the best. Usually, either the filament wire would burn out in only a few seconds or the glass bulb would burst, and Edison and his team would have to go back to the drawing board.

It took Edison and his men over a year of experimentation to find a filament wire that would conduct electricity long enough to be practical. For a long time, they experimented with platinum wires rolled in carbon, but these only burned for a few minutes. Then Edison made a carbonized strip of cardboard in the shape of a horseshoe, and put that inside the bulb, and it burned for about forty hours. Then he and his men experimented with wires made from various types of Japanese bamboo, and these burned even longer. Finally, a few years after he had patented the light bulb in 1881, Edison discovered that tungsten wires could burn for over 1000 hours inside a light bulb. He had perfected his product, as he said, through "99 percent perspiration," and tungsten wires are still used in light bulbs today.

> I have met many great thinkers, talkers, and planners, but very few people who could successfully execute their ideas on a consistent basis.

I have met many great thinkers, talkers, and planners, but very few people who could successfully execute their ideas on a consistent basis. One person who has influenced me a great deal is the author Jackie Collins, even though I have never read any of her books. I once saw her interviewed on a television talk show, in which she spoke about her book, *Hollywood Housewives*. After her book became a best seller, she said, people would come up to her at dinner parties or book signings, and say, "Oh, that was *my* book! I *could* have written that book! You took my ideas! I *should* have written that book!"

Ms. Collins said that she soon got very tired of hearing this. She resented the idea that other people thought that this should have been "their" book. She wanted to say to them, "No, this is *not* your book! This is *my* book! *I* was the one who got up at 4 AM every day, and worked fourteen-hour days for six months researching, writing, editing, and getting this book published. It is *mine*, not yours!"

I have never forgotten this interview with Jackie Collins. Her point is that an idea means absolutely nothing unless it is executed. An idea or concept will remain a dream unless you are willing to put in the long hours necessary to make your dream a reality. Many people may have indeed had an idea for a book about the romantic lives of housewives in Hollywood. Some of these people may have had access to the glamorous world and the Hollywood people that inspired the book. A few of them may have even had enough talent to write such a book. But only Jackie Collins was willing to sit down and put in the time and the sweat equity that it took to actually *write* it! As a result, *Hollywood Housewives* is *her* book, and she is a very wealthy person.

Execution is an absolute must for sustaining a business. As mundane as it sounds, execution is what keeps the business going. Jackie Collins has since written other best sellers. If *Hollywood Housewives* had been her only book, she would have been long forgotten by now. Her book made the *New York Times* Best Seller List because she had the talent to write a compelling book that could reach a wide audience. But her work ethic and her consistency in writing more books have *kept* her on this list. When people hear that Jackie Collins is coming out with a new book, they line up at the bookstores to buy it, because they know that she has written many other good books in the past.

Again, it's the same with business. If you have the initiative to start a business that delivers a useful product or service to your clients, they will remember that product or service. But if you *keep* delivering that useful product or service to your clients, they will always come back to you for more. But you must keep delivering that quality product or service time and again. You must *execute* your ideas or concepts consistently and efficiently. Remember, 82 percent of success is showing up.

THE RELIABILITY FACTOR

In this world, there are reliable people and unreliable people. As with everything, no one is 100 percent reliable or 100 percent unreliable. There is a wide gulf in between, but you should surround yourself with people you would share a foxhole with in a life-or-death situation. Succeeding in business will be so much easier if your efforts are supported by reliable people— or in other words, by people who show up.

As a business owner, you will quickly learn to distinguish the reliable associates from the unreliable ones. The reliable associates are those who always show up when you ask them to, and who deliver what you need from them time and again. The unreliable ones are those who show up late for meetings, miss deadlines, and turn in substandard work. The more you surround yourself with reliable people, the more your business will prosper. Of course, this assumes that *you* are a reliable person, and that you always complete your projects, turn in your best effort, show up for meetings on time, etc.

Answer this question honestly: Do you consider yourself a reliable person? Your answer will have a great bearing on whether or not you will succeed in business.

DELEGATE

If you can't delegate, it means…

a.   You are a lousy manager.

b.   You don't trust people.

c.   You can't communicate well with people, and therefore…

d.   You won't succeed in business

If you can't delegate, you will burn out sooner or later. Again, I believe that lack of organizational skills is the Number One reason why business owners "burn out." Not being able to delegate tasks is a close second. When you first start your business, you have a lot of extra energy because everything is so new. But eventually the novelty wears off. As your business grows, you soon find that you can't handle every task on every project all by yourself. Again, it will be better if you have some qualified free agents on hand to pick up the slack and take care of some of the more mundane tasks.

When I put together a radio ad campaign, almost all of the actual production work will be done by free agents. Once the client and I have determined the main concepts for the campaign, I call up one of my agents, a writer, and give them the concepts for the radio spots. At that point, *my* job is basically finished. The writer writes the radio spots and sends them on to another free agent, the producer. The producer produces the spots (with the help of other free agents to handle recording, voice-overs, and sound effects), and sends them back to the client for approval. If the client approves, another free agent then distributes the radio spots to a station. The producer then calls me to let me know that the project is complete.

Some people who have observed my business think that I should be more "in charge," that I should supervise more or actually be on hand when my free agents perform their duties. I prefer to treat people as professionals and to give my free agents plenty of room to succeed…or to fail. By placing my trust in them, I give them total responsibility. But more important, I make them totally accountable for their part in the process. If something goes wrong, I will know exactly where the problem is and I can deal with it on the spot. If people do not execute their tasks properly, I will replace them.

Like me, my free agents must be accessible. One requirement I have for all my free agents is that they must provide me with backup if they are not accessible for any reason. I don't care if the free agent who produces my radio spots goes on a six-month vacation to Australia, as long as he arranges a competent backup to take his place that will fully execute his tasks while he is gone. The burden is on him to make sure that there is no fall-off in the radio production area of my business. That goes for all of the free agents that work with me.

I provide most of my free agents with direct access to my clients. I monitor the contacts very closely, and I am always asking the client if they enjoy working with this or that free agent. If the response is yes, I probe further. I ask again if they *really* feel that way or if they are just trying to be cordial. I make it very clear that they should call me immediately if they are not 100 percent satisfied with the free agent's performance. Since I make sure that the people I work with are not only very competent but also have pleasant personalities, it is usually not a problem for my agents to contact my clients.

Luck is actually a very small factor on the road to success, no matter what your endeavor.

I have worked with too many people who over-supervise. Another term to describe these kinds of people is "control freaks." They want to be involved in *every* detail of *every* project. They stifle the creativity of the people who work for them, and more damaging, they slow down the process of getting the job done. This is not only annoying, it also hurts productivity. With control over every detail, it is impossible to determine who is really responsible for what aspect of the project. This type of management style may work (barely) in a corporate structure, but it won't work if you are trying to sustain your own business.

LUCK HAS LITTLE TO DO WITH SUCCESS

Every successful person will say that there was luck involved along their path to success. They got a break. Whether it is timing, or money that comes your way, or an unexpected opportunity, luck is actually a very small factor on the road to success, no matter what your endeavor.

Our national media focuses largely on the super-achievers—in sports, entertainment, business, politics, etc. When people comment on these super-achievers, I often hear them say: "They are gifted." "They were born that way." "They are just lucky." "They have a God-given ability." Nothing could be further from the truth.

Most super-achievers have three attributes in common. First, they have a strong role model (parent or adult) who coached them literally from the day they opened their eyes. Generally, the coach was focused on one goal: To make sure that the child would be the best at what they do. Tiger Woods had a golf club in his hands when he was two years old. His father had a tremendous influence on his development.

Second, and much more important, a super-achiever has a tremendous need and desire to succeed in a particular profession. While I was going out on dates and watching television as a teenager, the super-achievers were working many hours a day on their crafts. The sports kids were practicing their sports, the musicians were practicing their instruments or taking singing lessons, the software nerds were sitting at their computers designing basic computer programs, and so on.

Third, the super-achievers reach emotional and mental maturity a long time before other people in their age group. They attain many of the attributes expressed in this book at a very young age. In other words, super-achievers spend a good deal of the first part of their lives *putting themselves into a position to succeed.*

Every football team on the way to the Super Bowl has had one call or a bounce of the ball that goes their way. Without this one lucky bounce or call, they wouldn't be in the Super Bowl. It's often referred to as the "X factor" for the team. This lucky bounce may have come in a long-forgotten third game of the season, or in a playoff game, or in the actual Super Bowl itself.

But in truth, it is not so much luck as hard work and training that pays off. Yes, the ball may have taken a lucky bounce, but it was the team's hard training and the coach's direction that allowed them to be *in position* to catch the ball, or recover the fumble, or block the field goal kick and prevent the other team from scoring an extra three points to win the game. The football team is obviously exceptional in the first place to be a Super Bowl candidate. They have the talent that will put them in a position to take advantage of that lucky bounce.

We can't all be superstars. But through hard work and dedication, we can still put ourselves in a position to take advantage of opportunities when they come along. As I mentioned before, my big break came when a software company called me and asked if I did media buying. I had been slugging it out for ten years before I got "the call" that turned my business from a break-even communications company into a profitable enterprise. At first, I had a hard time accepting my good fortune. Then a friend reminded me of all those long hours and weekends I had spent building the business.

With my previous efforts—hosting my own radio show, selling radio spots to my newspaper clients—I had placed my business in a very good position to receive "the call" when it came. I was also flexible enough to change direction, so I could respond to the new client's needs immediately. If I'd had a partner, or was in debt, or hadn't been organized enough to take the call, I might not have been in a position to adjust so easily and quickly.

SELF-STARTER

Think about your life. Have you been one to stretch yourself, to look for ways to be more than you are? When you were in school, did you run for student council? Did you try out for a play, or for the cheerleading squad, or the football team, or perhaps the debate team? When you work for an employer, do you do the extra things to improve your job performance? If you work for the government, do you stay after 5 PM to make a good job better? Or is your attitude, "The government only has me 8 AM to 5 PM, period!"

If you have to ask why it is so important to be a self-starter, then starting a successful business will be very hard for you. If "82 percent of success is showing up," then the self-starters are the ones who add the extra "18 percent." In other words, self-starters do the extra things necessary to turn an average performance into an excellent performance. They are the ones who build their businesses from scratch, and who position themselves to be ready when opportunity comes along. The highest ranks of the successful in all industries—business, entertainment, sports, education—are made up of self-starters.

ACCESSIBILITY

As a self-employed business owner, you have a major advantage over large competitors in that you can provide your clients with *accessibility.* In a world that keeps driving people away from the human touch, the more accessible you are, the more people will want to do business with you. Being accessible to your clients is as much a part of the "82 percent of success is showing up" maxim as anything else.

> If "82 percent of success is showing up," then the self-starters are the ones who add the extra "18 percent." In other words, self-starters do the extra things necessary to turn an average performance into an excellent performance.

People are social. They want to deal with other people, and to be treated with respect. Nothing annoys them more than to call a major corporation and get a recording with a long list of menu choices, when all they need is an answer to a simple question. The larger the company (banks, airlines, phone companies, utilities, etc.), the harder it is to talk with an actual human being. Even if you do get through all the recorded menu options ("If you want to press one, press one! If you want to press two…"), it may only take you to voice-mail. ("I'm sorry. No one is available to take your call. Please leave a message after the tone.") Or even worse, it may take you *to no voice-mail at all!* ("We are experiencing a high volume of calls. Please try your call again later.")

Always make it easy for your clients to get a hold of you. Again, you can accomplish this with technology. Use one phone number for your office and cell phone, and have voice-mail in place on both. Check your voice-mail for messages frequently, and get back to your clients quickly. Returning phone calls promptly demonstrates to your clients that they are very important to you, and that you respect each individual caller. *Not* returning phone calls promptly speaks volumes about how you feel about your clients as well. Make each of your clients feel as if *they* are the only people that you are working for.

BUSINESS IS ABOUT THE MUNDANE

If "82 percent of success is showing up," then a good part of "showing up" is doing all those routine, everyday tasks that keep your business going. In the beginning, it will take a lot of hard work to get your business up and running. Starting a business is very time-consuming. For the first couple of years, you may have to work fifteen-hour days and weekends.

At some point, however, the effort that it takes to run your business will level out and things will start to run more smoothly. When you reach the point where you work eight-hour days, and a good part of your day is taken up by routine tasks such as making sales calls,

The more mundane your business becomes, the more successful it will be.

paying bills, and invoicing clients, you have reached the point of success in your business. The more mundane your business becomes, the more successful it will be.

I have seen too many businesses fail because their owners were too creative. They spent all their time sitting around dreaming about new concepts or creating new and innovative products that would help their clients. They couldn't be bothered with routine tasks, such as making sales calls or showing up on time for meetings. Unfortunately, these boring everyday "business" tasks are what keep the business going. I hate preparing tax returns, but paying taxes is more important for the survival of my business than sitting around trying to think up a breakthrough idea that may or may not come to fruition. The devil is in the details.

HEALTH

One final aspect of "showing up" is your health. Your good health or lack thereof has a lot to do with your long-term success in business. If you are frequently coming down with the flu, fevers, headaches, or severe colds, you might want to keep your day job and stay with an employer with good health insurance. Sustaining a business requires good health, because it requires daily attention. If you are unhealthy, it is not necessarily your fault, but it is a fact of life.

If you can find a way to hold on to your health insurance from your last corporate or government job, I highly recommend that you do it. When I first started my own business, I did without health insurance for a time to save money, but I *really* don't recommend this option to anyone else. Even if you and your family are considerably healthy, there is always the danger that an accident or sudden illness will occur, and then health insurance can be a lifesaver for you *and* your business.

To find out more about how a self-employed business owner can attain health insurance, contact your local chapter of the Small Business Administration. You can find the phone number for your local chapter at www.sba.gov, or call the national headquarters in Washington D.C. at: (202) 205-6605.

Conclusion

So there you have it. You now have a good idea of the emotional and personality traits that make up the self-employed mindset. You have seen how these traits often come into play in the self-employed lifestyle, and how they can affect the success or failure of your business. I hope that you now have some sense as to whether or not your own mindset will fit into that of the self-employed business owner.

From here, where you go is up to you. My advice is, be courageous, but use common sense. Pay attention to the principles I've outlined in this book, and you will give your business every chance to succeed.

Knowledge is power. The more you know about the way things *really* work in the world of self-employment, the better prepared you will be to face what lies ahead. I've given you what I have learned in my fifteen years as a business owner. What you learn from here is up to you.

I would very much like to hear from you if you found this book to be helpful in making your choice on whether or not to start your own business. I would also like to know if you've been able to apply any of the principles that I've outlined in this book to the everyday tasks of your own business.

You can contact me through e-mail at:
info@caseycommunications.net

I could end by saying, "Good luck!" But you and I both know that luck has very little to do with it.

FURTHER READING AND STUDY

The following books are great resources for starting a home-based business:

Working from Home, by Peter Hingston and Alstair Balfour.

Free Agent Nation, by Daniel H. Pink

The Business Start-Up Kit: Everything You Need to Know About Starting and Growing Your Own Business, by Steven D. Strauss

Home-Based Businesses for Dummies, by Paul & Sara Edwards.

Secrets of Self-Employment: Surviving and Thriving on the Ups and Downs of Being Your Own Boss, by Paul & Sara Edwards

The Entrepreneur's Desk Reference: Authoritative Information, Ideas, and Solutions for Your Small Business, by Jane Applegate

The Best Home Businesses for the 21st Century: The Inside Information You Need to Know to Select a Home-Based Business That's Right for You, by Paul & Sara Edwards.

Success For Less: 100 Low Cost Businesses You Can Start Today, by Rob & Terry Adams

Mompreneurs: A Mother's Practical Step-By-Step Guide to Work-At-Home Success by Ellen H. Parlapiano & Patricia Cobe

Self-Employment: From Dream to Reality! An Interactive Workbook for Starting Your Small Business, by Linda D. Gilkerson & Theresia M. Paauwe

The Economics of Self-Employment and Entrepreneurship, by Simon C. Parker

Thinking Like an Entrepreneur: How to Make Intelligent Business Decisions That Will Lead to Success in Building & Growing Your Own Company, by Peter I. Hupalo

What No One Ever Tells You About Starting Your Own Business: Real Life Start-Up Advice from 101 Successful Entrepreneurs, by Jan Norman

Starting on a Shoestring: Building a Business Without a Bankroll, by Arnold S. Goldstein

101 Tips for Running a Successful Home Business, by Maxye and Lou Henry.

The Work at Home Source Book, by Lynie Arden.

199 Great Home Businesses, by Tyler Hicks

And more resources...just before press time, I ran across the following two books.

The Innovators Solution, Professor Clayton Christensen, with Michael Raynor. Harvard School Press. (September, 2003)

Business gurus have long advocated that in order to succeed as an entrepreneur, you must simply find a way to build a better mousetrap. *The Innovators Solution* challenges that belief. Many businesses like Kodak and GladWare[1] have found new life because they actually made their products cheaper and easier to dispose of. Mr. Christensen is being hailed as "The Master of Innovation" and for good reason.

The Progress Paradox: How Life Gets Better, While People Feel Worse. Gregg Easterbrook. Random House

This is not a book about starting your own business but it does examine some very important questions that you should ask yourself before making the plunge. I spent a great deal of time in *Is Self-Employment for You?* asking you to examine the kind of lifestyle options you are seeking and if starting your own business is compatible with those goals. *The Progress Paradox* challenges the reader to examine the very same questions and much more.[2] Bottom line: There is more to life than acquiring things and you don't have to be in such a rush.

Paul Casey

[1]Information extracted from Newsweek Magazine article, November 17, 2003, pages E-6-E-10
[2]Information extracted from a Time Magazine article, December 15, 2003, pages 66-67

WEB SITES FOR FREE AGENTS AND ENTREPRENEURS

Free Agent Nation

http://www.freeagentnation.com/

Daniel H. Pink's own web site. Offers information on working for yourself, daily news updates, links to other free agents, and a free online newsletter.

Money-Making Mommies

http://www.moneymakingmommy.com/

Web site for mothers who would like to start home-based businesses.

Home-Based Jobs and Careers

http://www.jobs-central.com/homejobs.htm

Information on work-at-home-jobs and business opportunities

All Freelance

http://www.allfreelance.com/indexx.html

Features articles on getting started as a freelancer, how much to charge, promoting yourself, handling taxes, contracts, and money matters, and job listings.

Freelance Living

http://www.creativekeys.net/FreelanceLiving/flhome.html

A lifestyle guide for free agents and independent professionals. Includes articles and a newsletter on living and working as a freelancer.

WorkAtHomeIndex.net

http://www.work-at-home-index.net/

Work-at-home resources for home-business entrepreneurs. Includes very helpful articles on self-employment, traditional and Internet marketing, business opportunities, and telecommuting.

Entrepreneur.com

http://www.entrepreneur.com/

Features information for start-ups, home businesses, franchises, e-businesses, and articles about management, technology, sales, and marketing for small businesses.

SmartBiz.com

http://www.smartbiz.com/

Resources for small businesses. Includes pages on management, marketing and PR, sales, networking, and financing. Also offers standard business, legal, and tax forms.

Inc.com

http://www.inc.com/home/

Web site for *Inc.* magazine. Includes "How To" guides for business start-ups on getting started, sales, marketing, legal and tax matters, information technology, financing, e-commerce, and professional growth.

All Business

http://www.allbusiness.com/

Resources for small businesses. Includes a section of standard forms and agreements, a question-and-answer section for all types of small businesses, and a collection of business resource directories.

BizOffice.com

http://www.bizoffice.com/

Resources for small and home-based businesses. Includes news for entrepreneurs, financing opportunities, a reference section, and a section on applying for government grants.

MoreBusiness.com

http://www.morebusiness.com/

Web site with tips about starting and running a small business. Includes articles on marketing and financing, plus templates for contracts and agreements, free legal forms, and business checklists.

ATTITUDES, BELIEFS, EXPECTATIONS

Also, in Chapter Seven, "Judgment," I mentioned The Pacific Institute. Many of the qualities that it takes to successfully sustain a business are learned behaviors. The good news is that we have the ability to change our behaviors if some of them are negative and are holding us back.

The curriculum at The Pacific Institute teaches us that, as human beings with our cognitive powers, we are the sum total of our attitudes, beliefs, and expectations.

I have never found a better organization to provide an individual with the tools necessary to move to higher performance levels than The Pacific Institute. If you feel you may be lacking in some of the key traits it takes to sustain a business, I strongly recommend that you contact them. You can visit their web site at www.pac-inst.com.

You can also purchase a copy of Dr. Glenn Terrell's book, *The Ministry of Leadership, Heart & Theory*, at the Pacific Institute web site. This book is a great read and discusses, among other things, what the world of business really needs today: Leadership.

Order Form

QTY.	Title	Price
	Is Self-Employment for You?	$15.95
	Is Self-Employment for You? with CD	$25.90
	Shipping and Handling - Add $4.50 for orders in the US	
	CD only	$ 9.95
	Shipping and Handling - Add $2.00 for first CD. .50 for each additional CD	
	Sales tax (WA state residents only, add 8.8%)	
	Total enclosed	

Telephone Orders:
Call 1-800-461-1931
Have your Visa or
MasterCard ready.

Fax Order:
Fill out this form and fax it to:
425-398-1380

E-mail Orders:
harapub@foxinternet.net

Postal Orders::
Hara Publishing
P.O. Box 19732
Seattle, WA 98109

Payment Method (check one)
❑ Check
❑ Visa
❑ MasterCard

Name on card_____

Card #_____

Expiration Date_____Zip Code_____

Name_____

Address_____

City_____State_____Zip_____

Phone (   ) _____Fax_____

Quantity discounts available. Call (425) 398-2780
Thank you for your order!